SUSTAINABLE FACILITIES

About the Author

Keith Moskow is principal of Moskow Architects, a firm committed to sustainable and environmentally sensitive architecture. He has won awards from the American Institute of Architects, the Boston Society of Architects, the Municipal Arts Society of New York, the Centre for Critical Architecture, San Francisco, and AIA Chicago. Mr. Moskow is also the author of *Houses of Martha's Vineyard*.

SUSTAINABLE FACILITIES

Green Design, Construction, and Operations

Keith Moskow, AIA

New York   Chicago   San Francisco   Lisbon   London   Madrid   Mexico City   Milan   New Delhi   San Juan   Seoul   Singapore   Sydney   Toronto

The McGraw·Hill Companies

Cataloging-in-Publication Data is on file with the Library of Congress.

McGraw-Hill books are available at special quantity discounts to use as premiums and sales promotions, or for use in corporate training programs. To contact a representative please visit the Contact Us pages at www.mhprofessional.com.

1 2 3 4 5 6 7 8 9 0 WCK/WCK 0 1 2 1 0 9 8

ISBN 978- 0-07-149474-8
MHID 0-07-149474-X

 This book is printed on recycled, acid-free paper made from 100% postconsumer waste.

Sponsoring Editor	**Designer**
Joy Bramble Oehlkers	Lisa Erb
Acquisitions Coordinator	**Indexer**
Rebecca Behrens	Virginia Carroll
Editorial Supervisor	**Production Supervisor**
David E. Fogarty	Richard C. Ruzycka
Project Manager	**Composition**
Jan Bedger	North Market Street Graphics
Copy Editor	**Art Director, Cover**
Stewart Smith	Jeff Weeks

CONTENTS

ACKNOWLEDGMENTS

First and foremost, thanks to the contributing architects and their clients who supplied the vast majority of the photography and text for this publication. Thanks to my collaborators at Moskow Architects: Robert Linn, John Lodge, Jacqueline Maldonado, Cassandra Thornberg, and Will Morgan. Lastly, thanks to my wife, Allison, and my sons, Zac and Jake, who are supportive in every way.

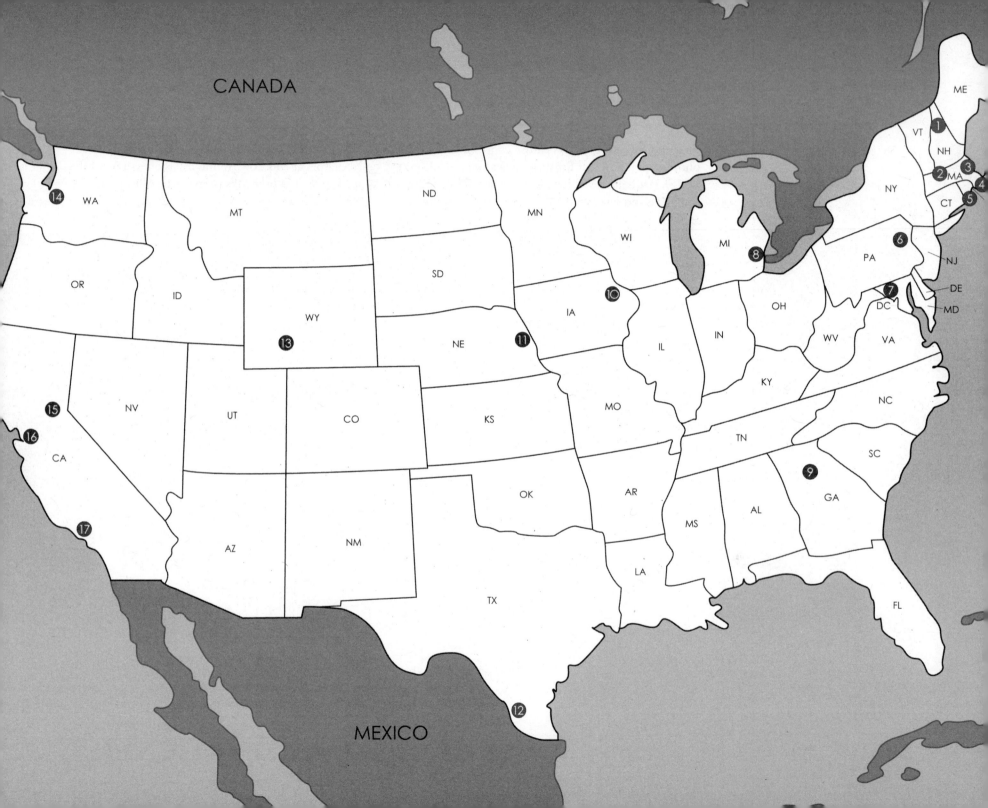

LEGEND

1. Appalachian Mountain Club,
   Crawford Notch, NH

2. The Doyle Conservation Center
   Leominster, MA

3. Conservation Law Foundation
   Boston, MA

4. Woods Hole Research Center
   Falmouth, MA

5. Bay Education Center
   Providence, RI

6. Pocono Environmental Education/Visitor Activity Center
   Dingmans Ferry, PA

7. Chesapeake Bay Foundation/Philip Merrill Environmental
   Center, Annapolis, MD

8. Kresge Foundation Building
   Troy, MI

9. Gwinnett Environmental & Heritage Center
   Buford, GA

10. Marion Art and Environmental Center
    Marion, IA

11. Carl T. Curtis National Park Service
    Omaha, NE

12. World Birding Center
    Mission, TX

13. National Outdoor Leadership School
    Headquarters, Lander, WY

14. IslandWood
    Bainbridge Island, WA

15. California Environmental Protection Agency
    Headquarters Building, Sacramento, CA

16. The Thoreau Center for Sustainability
    San Francisco, CA

17. The Robert Redford Building
    Santa Monica, CA

18. Forestech
    Baimsdale, Australia (Not Shown)

19. Federal Environmental Agency
    Dessau, Germany (Not Shown)

20. Institute for Forestry and Nature Research
    Wageningen, The Netherlands (Not Shown)

INTRODUCTION

It's not easy being green.

—Kermit the Frog

As concerns about global warming and oil prices mount, so too has interest in more sustainable, or green, construction—that is, developments that balance style and function with protection of the environment and conservation of natural resources.

—*The New York Times,* April 29, 2007

As sustainability becomes an increasingly important aspect of architecture and construction, many environmental organizations have used their need for new buildings as a way to champion "green" design. This book features case studies of 20 significant projects designed for environmental organizations. In each case, the architects and their clients have integrated both their functional requirements and a wide range of sustainable strategies into the architecture. The result is more than a collection of good buildings designed for well-meaning groups: the projects

PROJECT 1 Appalachian Mountain Club, Crawford Notch, NH

PROJECT 2 The Doyle Conservation Center, Leominster, MA

PROJECT 3 Conservation Law Foundation, Boston, MA

PROJECT 4 Woods Hole Research Center, Falmouth, MA

presented here offer objective, educational examples of how green design can help us not only become more responsible stewards of our environment, but also create demonstrably better architecture.

The term *sustainable* has become thoroughly ingrained in the lexicon of architecture and construction. The specifications for many new buildings—particularly those for public agencies or institutional clients—carry catchphrases such as *green, sustainable, energy efficient,* and *LEED-certified.* These labels are very recent, while Earth Day, perhaps the most popular recognition of global environmental issues, is only 40 years old. Sustainable architecture itself, however, is as old as man the builder—to take just one example, consider the Anasazi tribe's dwellings in the American Southwest. The Leadership in Environmental and Energy Design (LEED) certification process is essentially an acknowledgment of and return to age-old methods of working in harmony within a specific environment. A sustainable design program fashioned by the U.S. Green Building Council, LEED was first implemented in 2000 and is now a standard for any building overseen by the General Services Administration.

More important, the idea of green as a practical and economic response to climate change is taking hold in the public consciousness. Vice President Al Gore not only won an Academy Award for *An Inconvenient Truth,* a documentary on global warming, but was awarded the Nobel Peace Prize for his efforts to rally the world to respond responsibly to climate change. For too long, the American people were not ready to acknowledge the effects of bad stewardship of the natural resources and take the steps necessary to confront the problems. Now, the message has been brought home to us by scientists, environmentalists,

PROJECT 5 Bay Education Center, Providence, RI

PROJECT 6 Pocono Environmental Education/Visitor Activity Center, Dingmans Ferry, PA

PROJECT 7 Chesapeake Bay Foundation/Philip Merrill Environmental Center, Annapolis, MD

PROJECT 8 Kresge Foundation Building, Troy, MI

PROJECT 9 Gwinnett Environmental & Heritage Center, Buford, GA

PROJECT 10 Marion Arts and Environmental Center, Marion, IA

PROJECT 11 Carl T. Curtis National Park Service, Omaha, NE

PROJECT 12 World Birding Center, Mission, TX

and, not least of all, architects. The architecture profession, with all its related disciplines, will be required to spearhead meaningful change in the standards of efficiency and sustainability in the building industry.

As a practicing architect, my first opportunity to introduce sustainability into the design process on a large scale came in 1993 when the Conservation Law Foundation (CLF) set about building a new headquarters in Boston that would help them practice what they preached. The CLF, which was founded in 1966, has made a name for itself as a protector of the environment through advocacy. Their successes include laws that regulate lead paint, restrictions designed to save North Atlantic fisheries, the ongoing cleanup of Boston Harbor, and the restoration of the region's air quality.

The new headquarters, a renovated four-story Italianate commercial block, was designed to show how such a makeover could make good business sense. The space needed to be energy efficient, be constructed of environmentally friendly materials, and pay for itself in five years. The CLF's space was conceived not as a glorified science experiment, but as a comfortable, cost-effective headquarters that could serve as a model for other organizations.

The foundation's mission was an internal success. As promised, the new headquarters—which was designed and built using a holistic approach that incorporates energy efficient heating and cooling, daylighting, passive ventilation, and recycled and sustainable materials—paid for itself within five years. This success garnered the project the first Boston Society of Architects Sustainable Design Honor Award. Unfortunately, however, the building's success had little impact within the local institutional community because CLF had no viable way to promote the project beyond their immediate group of constituents.

A decade later, we designed a building addition for CLF that became the third building in Massachusetts to receive LEED certification (Project 3). The certification itself represented a significant advance in the development of sustainable design standards. However, once again, despite CLF's initiative for others to use CLF's green design as a model, the project did little to encourage more mainstream organizations to introduce sustainability in their own building. Many environmental organizations like the CLF are addressing both the challenges and the potential of sustainable design in their own projects both nationally and internationally; however, their efforts have not been widely disseminated. Now is the time for them to be recognized. Thus, CLF and all the other environmental groups that practice what they preach became the inspiration for this book as a vehicle to make the results of their successes available to the widest possible audience.

For this book we solicited submissions of distinguished architecture by and for environmental organizations through institutional and ad hoc channels. We were happily surprised by the response of over 80 quality submissions. In the search for the good and the green, we considered a wide range of criteria that include scale, budget, both new construction and renovation, and a variety of locations (urban, rural, suburban). We also put a special emphasis on performance because as these concepts percolate down to the wider construction world, the most important message to deliver is that sustainable design makes better buildings.

As we narrowed down the field, it became abundantly clear that sustainable design is not a style, but an approach—an ethic, not an aesthetic. At the same time, a sustainable design vocabulary does emerge.

PROJECT 13 National Outdoor Leadership School Headquarters, Lander, WY

PROJECT 14 IslandWood, Bainbridge Island, WA

PROJECT 15 California Environmental Protection Agency Headquarters Building, Sacramento, CA

PROJECT 16 The Thoreau Center for Sustainability, San Francisco, CA

PROJECT 17 The Robert Redford Building, Santa Monica, CA

PROJECT 18 Forestech, Baimsdale, Australia

PROJECT 19 Federal Environmental Agency, Dessau, Germany

PROJECT 20 Institute for Forestry and Nature Research, Wageningen, The Netherlands

This is particularly evident in the way these buildings respond to their sites and the local climates. In addition to the innovations and ideas presented in the projects shown here, we also note that a number of organizations, both governmental and private, have started to have a substantial impact on the way other structures are being built. Specifically, the Department of Energy's Energy Star rating system and the United States Green Building Council's LEED rating system, as well as a number of high-profile local and state government programs, have done a great deal to raise the profile of sustainable design and construction and to make it more affordable. At the same time, more and more universities are making commitments to build sustainably. This is not surprising, since these institutions look at the performance of their projects over a much longer time period than many commercial owners.

The goal of *Sustainable Facilities: Green Design, Construction, and Operations* is to provide compelling examples of sustainable design that both inspire and educate. A second and equally important concept the book addresses is that green design is good business: sustainable developments are more cost-effective in the long term and, therefore, ultimately, more valuable.

SUSTAINABLE FACILITIES

APPALACHIAN MOUNTAIN CLUB, HIGHLAND LODGE AND EDUCATION CENTER
CRAWFORD NOTCH, NEW HAMPSHIRE

Completed:	October 2003
Owner:	Appalachian Mountain Club Andrew Falender, Executive Director Walter Graff, Deputy Director Paul Cunha, Director of Facilities
Architects:	Carlone Dick LaFleche Dennis Carlone, Architect & Master Planner Douglas Dick, Architect Dean Hofelich, Project Manager
Consultants:	H. E. Bergeron Engineers—Civil Engineers Kohler & Lewis—Mechanical and Plumbing Engineers LeMessurier Consultants—Structural Engineers Downing Engineering—Electrical Engineers Energysmiths—Sustainable Design Advisor Halvorson Design Partnership, Inc.—Landscape Architects & Master Planner
General Contractor:	MacMillin Company, Keene, New Hampshire
Photographer:	Peter Vanderwarker
Site:	The center is located on an historic 26-acre site in the White Mountains of New Hampshire.
Environment:	Rural

Program: Environmental Education Center and Lodge Complex including dormitory, offices, and conference spaces

Square Footage:
38,000 square feet—Highland Lodge
11,700 square feet—Thayer Hall
880 square feet—Garn Building
915 square feet—Maintenance Building
51,495 square feet—Total

Structural System:
- Steel frame is 95 percent recycled steel fabricated 45 miles from the site
- Dining room timber framing from a pier in Oregon
- Crushed existing asphalt used on new parking lot and roadway

Mechanical System:
- Biomass central boiler by Garn
- Heat recovery boilers and water heaters
- Two biodiesel backup boilers
- Low-flow toilets in Highland Lodge
- Composting toilets in Thayer Hall and railroad depot

Materials:
- Insulspan structural insulated panels (SIPs) on roof and walls
- Nu-Wool cellulose wall insulation at Thayer Hall
- Triple-glazed low-emissivity (low-E) fiberglass windows
- Thermally broken aluminum entry doors
- Polyurethane foam sealant on doors and windows
- Mineral wood sound bats
- 89 percent recycled content carpeting by Shaw
- Coated steel standing seam roofing by Integris
- Low volatile organic compound (low-VOC) paint in guest rooms
- Gypsum wall board, 95 percent recycled content

Low-maintenance landscaping—native wildflowers located outside the dining area and throughout the main site are irrigation-free and maintain the natural consistency of the White Mountains.

PROJECT DESIGN

"Founded in 1876, the Appalachian Mountain Club, a nonprofit organization with more than 90,000 members, promotes the protection, enjoyment, and wise use of the mountains, rivers, and trails of the Appalachian region. We believe that the mountains and rivers have an intrinsic worth and also provide recreational opportunity, spiritual renewal, and ecological and economic health for the region. We encourage people to enjoy and appreciate the natural world because we believe that successful conservation depends on this experience."

—The Appalachian Mountain Club Mission Statement.

In keeping with its core mission, when the Appalachian Mountain Club (AMC) decided to upgrade its Crawford Notch campus, it commissioned a design team to generate a sustainable master plan that integrated the disparate program elements of education, housing, lodging, and offices into a coherent whole. This plan included a detailed analysis of program needs and existing historic structures; an integrated and sustainable approach to site planning, architecture, and engineering; and an estimate of project costs. Once this master plan was completed, the architects assembled a project team that included both AMC staff members and board members.

Following a longtime AMC tradition, the design favors sensible, functionally proven, and cost-effective green technology over expensive, experimental green approaches. While a majority of the center's visitors come during the summer, it is active throughout the year. Given the harsh winter conditions—winds can reach as high as 100 miles per hour and the valley gets 13 feet of snow annually—the buildings' envelopes had to be designed to deal with these extremes. The result is a complex of six buildings that combines careful massing and siting with a rugged vernacular that is sympathetic to the renovated structures. The overall project has a cohesive and unself-conscious feel that is appropriate both to the Appalachian Mountain Club's institutional image and to Crawford Notch's natural beauty.

PROJECT CONSTRUCTION

The local climate clearly pointed to the need for a well-insulated and airtight skin. Highland Lodge has 6½-inch wall and 8½-inch roof wrap of panelized insulation and triple-glazed fiberglass single-hung windows. A centralized Garn biomass boiler, which cleanly burns locally harvested cord wood, scraps, and pallets, is the heart of the hot water in the multiple building heating system. Additional heat from ventilation exhaust and kitchen hot water use is harvested back to the buildings' heating system.

The ventilation system is designed to maximize fresh air intake, and almost all interior finishes contain no volatile organic compounds (VOCs). Efficient building lighting augments good daylighting, which is achieved through a shallow building depth, interior windows, and an east–west orientation. Site lighting minimizes light spill onto adjacent areas and maintains a dark sky. The complex uses state-of-the-art septic and nitrogen removal systems.

THIS PAGE LEFT: The dining room features timber columns reclaimed from a harbor pier in Portland, Oregon.

THIS PAGE TOP RIGHT: Thayer Community Room.

THIS PAGE BOTTOM RIGHT: Looking into the Great Room.

OPPOSITE PAGE: The Great Room offers guests interaction with lodge tradition in the spirit of its historic structure.

PROJECT USE

The Highland Center contains three new buildings (Highland Lodge and Environmental Center, Garn Building, and Maintenance Structure), one restored structure (Thayer Hall), and two existing buildings (AMC's Shapleigh Studio and one nearby private cabin). An historic Railroad Station Visitor Center and its new adjoining structure (designed by others) are 600 feet to the south. All public structures and the site have green design exhibits that are part of both formal and informal tours. This campus layout allows both the public and the staff to share the complex's amenities in an informal, but effective, way.

The Highland Lodge, the largest structure of the complex, contains areas dedicated to environmental education, overnight lodging, dining/kitchen facilities, communal spaces, and support areas. The ground floor contains two teaching rooms, one workshop/breakout meeting room, lodge/hostel front desk, lobby, living room, small and large dining rooms (120 guests) with related kitchen/server spaces, service dock, small trading post, and ample circulation with informal meeting places. The first floor has five connections to the exterior including three covered porches and landscape meeting places. The second and third floors house both hostel rooms and lodge rooms. The second floor has a library, and the third floor has a parlor. The basement contains a future recreation room, storage for teaching/camping equipment, laundry, kitchen storage, and utilities.

Thayer Hall, a 100-year-old hotel carriage house, required complete reconstruction; only the timber frame and brick pavers were reusable. Thayer Hall also houses multiple uses that include education, administration, meeting/conferences, exhibits, and staff

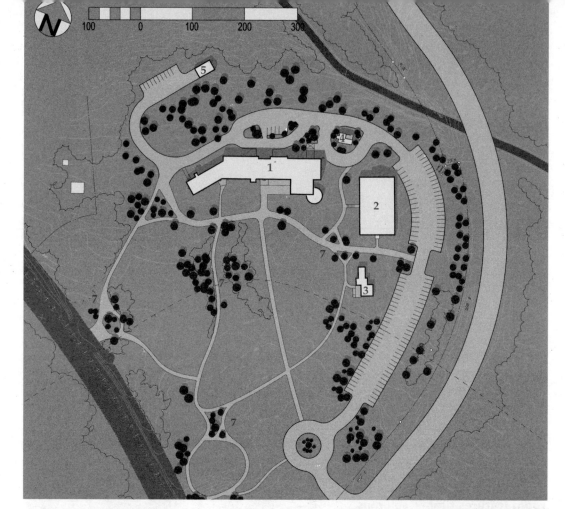

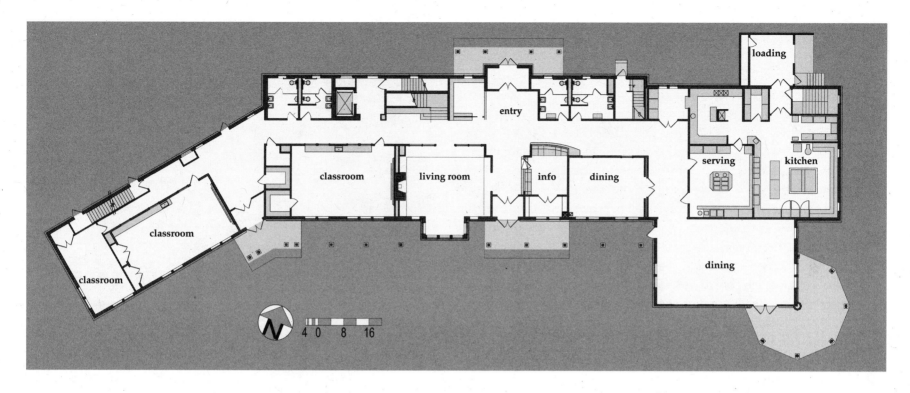

Ground-floor plan with labels: loading, entry, serving, kitchen, classroom, classroom, classroom, living room, info, dining, dining

4 0 8 16

ABOVE: Ground-floor plan of the Highland Center.

OPPOSITE: Site plan.

housing. The hall's main central space serves as a large meeting/conference space for 200 people. Two seminar teaching rooms, AMC staff offices, related support spaces, and a separate building entry suite for staff housing encircle the main central space on the first floor. Staffing is primarily on the second floor.

As the name implies, the Garn Building is a new structure housing the wood-fueled Garn biomass boiler, which provides heat and hot water for the lodge, Thayer Hall, and future structures. The small structure also has room for multiple-day wood storage, which is replenished as needed. There is also a maintenance building that is separated but visible from the center core. It houses AMC's construction and maintenance equipment and a small workshop. In addition, composting takes place just outside of the structure.

The Shapleigh Studio, the former painting studio of landscape painter Frank Henry Shapleigh, was relocated onto a new foundation and is now utilized as a library, meeting space, and studio for an artist or academic in residence.

The Carriage House restoration transformed a decaying 11,400-square-foot, timber-frame carriage house into an energy efficient, light-filled, multiuse building. The main central space, the Washburn Gallery, also provides an assembly room for 200 people. The perimeter spaces house AMC offices and conference/teaching rooms, and the second level provides dormitory rooms for AMC staff. The main building entry remains below the dormer. Separate staff offices and dormitory entrances were located to separate possible use conflicts.

BIOMASS BOILER

There are a number of reasons why a biomass boiler is appropriate for the Appalachian Mountain Club. First, using sustainably harvested wood, in concert with replanting trees in a managed forestry operation, moves toward carbon neutral energy production as opposed to adding to CO_2 levels utilizing fossil fuels. Second, in New Hampshire, wood is a locally produced fuel; thus, both transportation costs and the transportation-related use of fossil fuels are reduced. Biomass energy production also puts into practice one of AMC's environmental efforts related to their Maine Woods Initiative. The initiative is dedicated to addressing regional economic and ecological needs through outdoor recreation, resource protection, sustainable forestry, and community partnerships. Specifically, it develops markets for sustainably harvested forestry products. Finally, the biomass boiler is a practical, dependable, and proven sustainable energy technology.

The Highland Center heating plant is a nonpressurized, energy-storing wood-burning boiler called a Garn boiler. The combustion chamber, which can burn split wood and logs as well as scrap wood, is sealed and surrounded by a nonpressurized jacket of water that is heated and distributed to heat exchangers in the various buildings it serves. The water jacket also serves as a thermal storage feature that allows the boiler to maintain the system's designed water temperature range in between scheduled stokings of the boiler. Depending on fuel, the Garn boiler at the Highland Center is rated at 950,000 Btu/hr and has a storage capacity of 2,064,000 Btu (120 to 200°). With regard to emissions, the results of the 2006 test indicate that Garn has a particulate emission rate of 0.297 lb per 1,000,000 Btu input. This is 51 percent *below* the proposed performance level for Phase I of the EPA voluntary program for hydronic wood-fired heaters. This program specifies a maximum particulate emission of 0.6 lb per 1,000,000 Btu input. The Garn boiler produces an average of 15,000,000 Btu of heat from one cord of seasoned red oak (average of about 86 percent efficiency).

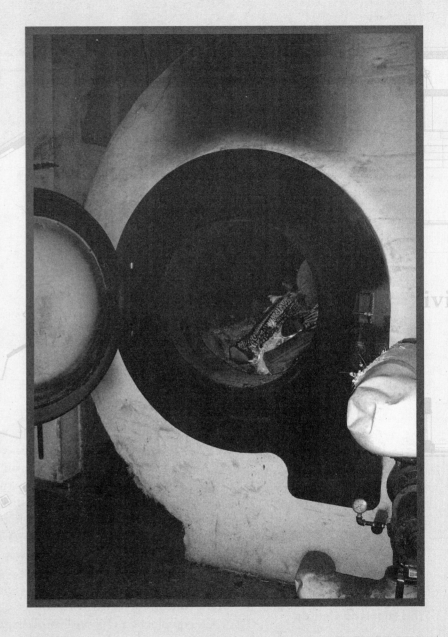

The system design for the Highland Center uses a central wood-fired biomass Garn boiler that heats three separate structures. The buildings are interconnected with a buried, highly insulated glycol heating loop. In each structure is a heat exchanger that transfers heat to a hot water fin-tube delivery system.

The biomass boiler is housed in a stand-alone boiler building with room for storing several cords of wood for seasoning and easy access for feeding the boiler. The stand-alone boiler building also houses the emergency electric generator (fueled with locally sourced biodiesel) and is the main distribution center for electricity throughout the Highland Center. This design allows for future use of the biomass boiler to function as an electrical cogeneration plant, which AMC envisions as producing more efficient and dependable electricity, in lieu of fossil fuel–generated and not always dependable electricity provided by the local power utility. Each building has its own biodiesel-fueled backup boiler to provide a redundant heating system. The modular biodiesel boilers work in tandem with the wood boiler supplying the last 10 percent of heating demand, allowing the biomass boiler to operate at its maximum efficiency even when heating and hot water demand is not at its maximum.

There are some unique challenges associated with the Garn system. The biomass boiler system is not an autofeed system like a wood chip or pellet biomass boiler, which feature hopper-style continuous fuel feeding. Instead, it is fueled much like a residential wood stove. The boiler must be opened and manually fed firewood, logs, or scrap lumber up to 48 inches. AMC made the decision to utilize the manual feed approach of the Garn with the understanding that the additional labor costs would be offset by lower fuel costs. Also, the process of stoking the boiler fits the historic image of the AMC that embodies an active, outdoors lifestyle.

The biomass boiler building design is important in making the storage and handling of wood very efficient. The goal is to reduce the number of times that the wood is actually handled. The staff brings bins or pallets of wood into the building with a tractor, sliding it in through an overhead door and positioning the bins so that staff moves the wood directly from the bin into the boiler.

Wood storage is another challenging aspect of utilizing a wood biomass boiler in this location, given the area's high snowfall, high wind, and low winter temperatures. The Highland Center utilizes over 50 cords of wood during a heating season. This wood, if stored on-site, needs to be covered and easily accessible to move into the biomass boiler building for use. In the severe winter microclimate at Crawford Notch in the White Mountains, wood must be under shelter in order to be available and in usable condition during the heating season. If left outdoors, the wood would be buried in snow and ice, resulting in inefficient fuel. Rather than building a separate structure for storing and stacking loose firewood, the AMC has developed a wood purchase/delivery system with scheduled deliveries of pallet cordwood minimizing the amount of wood stored on-site.

The Garn biomass boiler is most effective and efficient when running at high temperatures, so the engineering team purposely undersized the biomass boiler capacity so that when heating requirements are lower, the boiler is still running at close to peak capacity. During higher heating load conditions, the biodiesel modular backup boilers provide the extra capacity. The initial year of operation showed that running the biomass boiler at lower temperatures resulted in less efficient use of wood and more smoke output.

Prevailing winds were taken into consideration in the positioning of the boiler building to minimize smoke intake into the building's fresh air intake louvers and windows, which might be open during transitional seasons. Although efficient and clean burning, biomass boilers burning cord wood still create some amount of smoke and the smell of burning wood.

THE DOYLE CONSERVATION CENTER

LEOMINSTER, MASSACHUSETTS

Completed:	2004
Owner:	The Trustees of Reservations
Architecture:	HKT Architects Inc. W. Eric Kluz AIA LEED AP (Principal Architect) Zeljko Toncic AIA, LEED AP (Project Manager/Architect) Marta Kabalin, AIA, LEED AP (Interior Design Architect)
Consultants:	Beals & Thomas, Inc.—Civil Engineering Souza True and Partners, Inc.—Structural Engineering Arup—MEP Engineering Global Resource Options—Alternative Energy Design & Contracting Hines Wasser & Associates LLC—Landscape Architecture
Contractor:	Mullaney Corporation
Photographer:	Dan Gair/Blind Dog Photo (DG) Frank Siteman, courtesy of the Trustees of Reservations (FS)
Site:	Within a 200+ acre nature preserve, the building is clustered behind a New England saltbox home and extended garage complex on a road with a country lane flavor.
Environment:	Rural

The various parts of the center are organized to create a large courtyard. This serves as a focal point for public activities during temperate months. (FS)

Program:	The building's offices and meeting rooms serve as the organization's central regional office and house statewide resource protection programs and the Putnam Conservation Institute, an initiative formed to increase the capacity of the conservation community to protect, care for, and interpret the natural and cultural resources of Massachusetts.

Square Footage: 18,000 square feet

Sustainable Features:
- Sustainable site
- Sited at previously disturbed area
- Small building footprint to maximize open space
- Minimum parking spaces required by zoning
- Bicycle storage and changing rooms promote use of alternative transportation
- Bioswale constructed for stormwater treatment and management
- 90 percent of building receives daylight, with views to the outdoors
- Composting toilets
- Low flow faucets and urinals
- Gray water recycling system
- Landscaping designed with native vegetation and no need for irrigation

Structural System:
- Frame: reinforced concrete foundation wall, recycled structural steel, glue-laminated structural columns and beams
- Floor: concrete slab on grade
- Roof: prefabricated roof trusses, structural insulated roof panels (over basilica)

Mechanical System:
- 2,000 feet of roof-mounted photovoltaic cells provide 25 percent of building's electricity
- Mixed mode HVAC operation with automatic window openers for natural ventilation
- Ground source heat pump system for heating and cooling, using two injection-type open wells
- Energy recovery unit with enthalpy heat wheel on ventilation systems
- Heat management system to regulate indoor air temperature with the lowest energy costs
- Compact fluorescent smart lights automatically adjust to lighting needs

BELOW: Site plan.

Sustainable Materials:

- Bamboo and cork flooring
- Desks and shelving made of agricultural by-products
- Siding made from by-product of hardwood timber harvesting
- Carpet tiles made from recycled fibers
- Fabric on acoustic tiles in cubicles made from recycled fabric
- Landscaping and foundation stone harvested on-site
- Mulch from stumps from site preparation
- Local wood used where possible

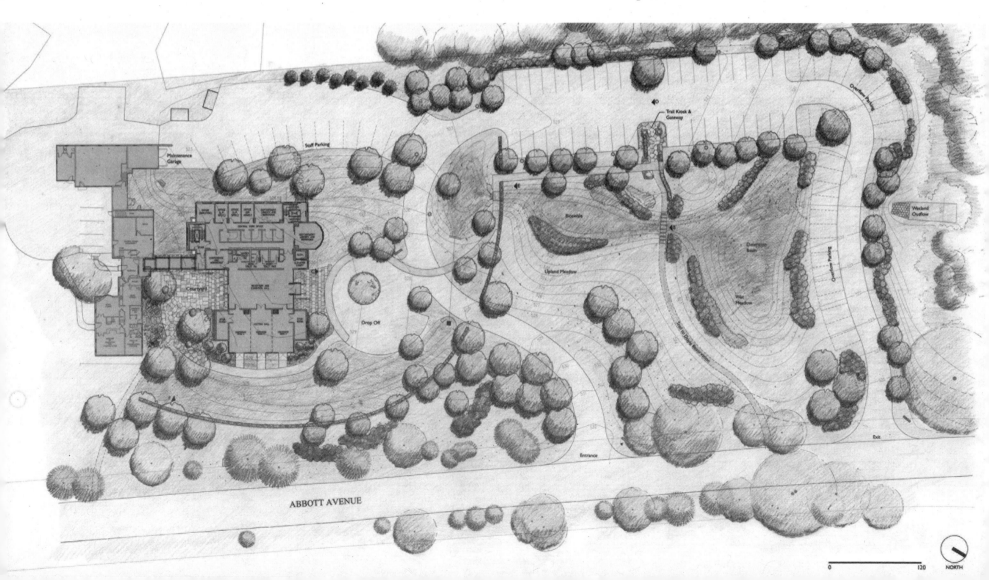

ABBOTT AVENUE

0   120   NORTH

PROJECT DESIGN

The Doyle Conservation Center is the first capital project undertaken by the Trustees of Reservations. One of the first decisions of the design team and the trustees was to work with the U.S. Green Building Council's LEED rating system. Together, they set an ambitious goal of achieving a Gold certification level for the building. As early adopters of the LEED system, the Trustees' pursuit of such a high degree of sustainability required a remarkable commitment, especially given the tight budget and the limited availability of green materials and technologies. However, the organization felt that, given its 100+-year-old commitment to the environment, it was important to take an approach to this capital project that is consistent with the Trustees of Reservations' core mission.

The 18,000-square-foot building is located in a nature preserve within an extensive second-growth forest. A previously disturbed site was selected for the new construction. The materials, colors, and textures recall the vernacular of the traditional architecture. The building's massing is broken down into discrete parts that are not seen from the street. As visitors turn down the drive alongside the original saltbox, the new building unfolds gradually. The parking lots are the minimum size required by city zoning. The design goal was to keep the scale of the building small and to maximize the open space around it.

The design team shared a broad exposure to holistic green building concepts and a commitment to incorporate them wherever possible. This created a collaborative atmosphere that allowed for a much more interactive design process. For example, when the architects derived the basic forms from the area's historical precedents, this inspired the mechanical engineers to propose an equally derivative automatic ventilation system that relies on natural currents and temperature gradients.

This holistic approach is also seen in the combination of strategies used to minimize the building's overall energy requirements. Roof-mounted photovoltaic panels provide 25 percent of the building's electricity, and two 1,500-foot geothermal wells provide heating and cooling without the use of on-site fossil fuels. Indoor air quality is assured with an intelligent ventilation system and operable windows. Water is conserved by low-flow fixtures and the use of composting toilets. In total, the building is 61.2 percent more efficient to power, heat, and cool than other buildings of an equivalent size and uses and consumes less water.

The site design by Hines Wasser & Associates features a circular wall constructed from stones harvested on-site. The wall connects the building and landscape and serves as seating for informal outdoor use. Use of indigenous plants eliminates the need for irrigation and the man-made wetland and meadow are designed to capture and filter stormwater runoff and recharge the watershed.

All offices have views to the outdoors. The interior workspaces have borrowed daylight from glazed side panels and transoms. (DG)

PROJECT CONSTRUCTION

Many of the building's materials were selected specifically for resource efficiency. The exterior siding, as well as the casework and furniture, were made from agricultural and wood by-products. The flooring is either cork or bamboo, both of which are rapidly renewable products.

Exterior looking southeast. The exterior of the center features high-performance insulated panel walls and roofs. The thermal performance values are R-27 and R-30, respectively.

The dining room features timber columns reclaimed from a harbor pier in Portland, Oregon.

The main meeting hall is divisible by three, with seating for a total of 150 people and includes comprehensive audiovisual capabilities. The room also opens to a landscaped terrace for receptions with casual seating available on the circular stone wall.

The exterior massing, the siting, and the landscape plan were designed to minimize the center's impact on its surroundings.

The fourth floor conference room is flooded by natural light from above. Cork interior walls attenuate sound transmission.

The Conservation Law library stacks are integrated into the second, third, and fourth floor halls. Natural light is borrowed from adjacent offices.

WOODS HOLE RESEARCH CENTER, GILMAN ORDWAY CAMPUS
FALMOUTH, WOODS HOLE, MASSACHUSETTS

View of addition exterior from the north.

Stairs showing daylighting scheme.

View of the Bay Education Center from southeastern shore.

Lobby floor with laser-cut linoleum map of Narragansett Bay for children's educational uses.

View of the center's south facade at night.

Manual devices rather than automated systems supplement natural approaches in the design of a mechanical system. Users make direct energy choices in this one-to-one connection with nature and its built environment.

Headquarters view across the Chesapeake Bay from the west, showing entry and rainwater cisterns.

Organized in four quadrants, two on each floor, the headquarters' double height lobby and exhibit space functions as an interactive node for both employees and visitors alike.

ABOVE: The connector—a covered walkway makes an indoor–outdoor connection with the outdoors as staff and conference attendees use outdoor spaces for informal gatherings. (DG)

RIGHT: The main meeting hall is divisible by three, with seating for a total of 150 people and includes comprehensive audiovisual capabilities. The room also opens to a landscaped terrace for receptions with casual seating available on the circular stone wall. (DG)

Indoor air quality was also a major area of concern with regard to materials—the long-term health effects of buildings on their occupants is increasingly recognized as an important issue. Consequently, most of the furnishings are made of recycled and natural materials that cause little off-gassing of toxic fumes. The paints, glues, and varnishes throughout the building were chosen for their low levels of volatile organic VOCs.

As early proponents of sustainable design and early adopters of the LEED initiative, the client and the design and construction team were faced with a challenging learning curve. While most of the principles of green building were fairly straightforward, business was not as usual and decisions needed to be made carefully. Though the programming objectives remained clear, the development of an integrated approach to the green elements of design required the client, designers, and contractors to work together to educate each other.

This was especially true with regard to documentation. Although the construction managers were engaged early in the design process, their initial focus was primarily on cost containment (their area of expertise) rather than on issues related to sustainability. Thus, when it came time for the actual construction, the documentation and methods required by LEED came as a bit of a surprise to both the design team and the builder. Although the team was successful in meeting the requirements for the Gold level of certification, much of the documentation, in particular that involving construction issues, had to be reconstructed after the fact.

A lesson learned is that one member of the construction team needs to be in charge of the reporting and documentation requirements, on-site manage-

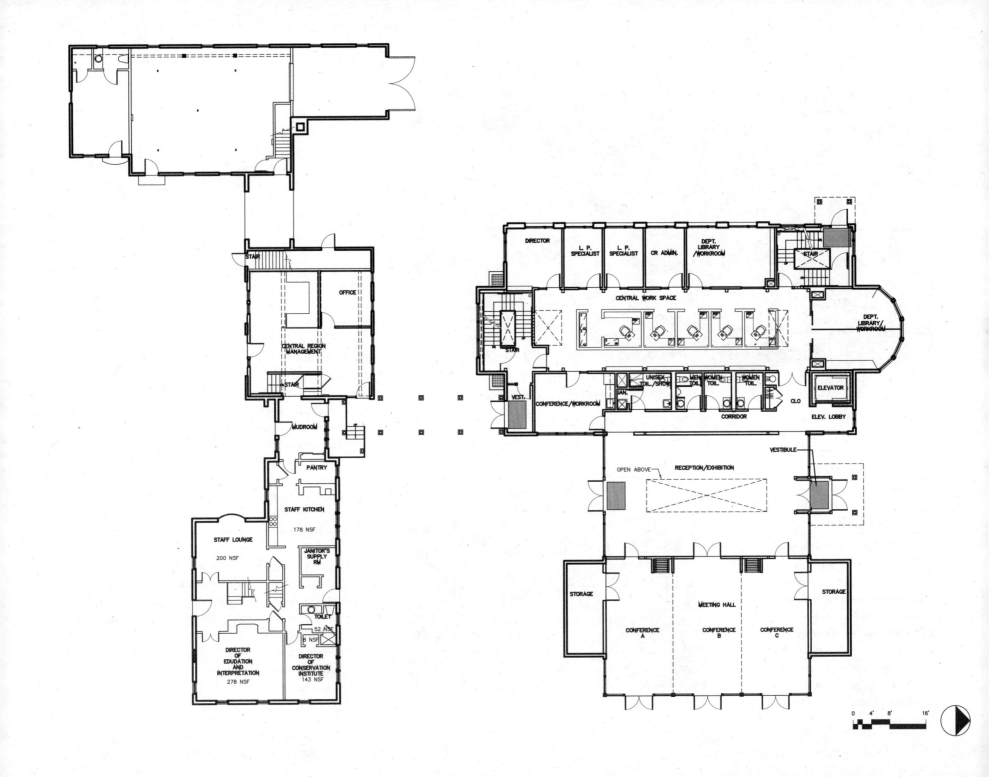

STAIR

OFFICE

CENTRAL REGION
MANAGEMENT

STAIR

MUDROOM

PANTRY

STAFF KITCHEN

178 NSF

STAFF LOUNGE

200 NSF

JANITOR'S
SUPPLY
RM

TOILET

52 NSF

8 NSF

DIRECTOR
OF
EDUCATION
AND
INTERPRETATION

278 NSF

DIRECTOR
OF
CONSERVATION
INSTITUTE

143 NSF

DIRECTOR

L. P.
SPECIALIST

L. P.
SPECIALIST

CR ADMIN.

DEPT.
LIBRARY
/WORKROOM

STAIR

CENTRAL WORK SPACE

STAIR

DEPT.
LIBRARY/
WORKROOM

VEST.

CONFERENCE/WORKROOM

JAN.

UNISEX
TOIL/SHOW

MEN
TOIL.

WOMEN
TOIL.

WOMEN
TOIL.

CLO

ELEVATOR

CORRIDOR

ELEV. LOBBY

VESTIBULE

OPEN ABOVE

RECEPTION/EXHIBITION

STORAGE

MEETING HALL

STORAGE

CONFERENCE
A

CONFERENCE
B

CONFERENCE
C

0   4'   8'   16'

THIS PAGE: Building section north-south through the basilica.

OPPOSITE PAGE: First-floor plan.

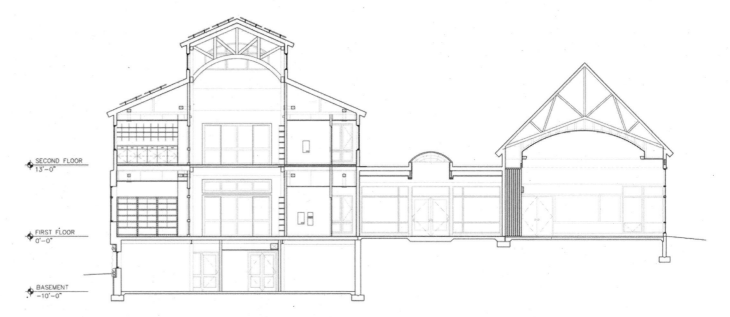

SECOND FLOOR
13'-0"

FIRST FLOOR
0'-0"

BASEMENT
-10'-0"

ment and protection of materials, and the flow of construction waste.

The second important lesson involves commissioning. A commissioning agent was engaged once the building was finished, and he uncovered a number of issues that needed to be addressed. Had the commissioning agent been included from the beginning, during the design phase, there may have been a better overlap of accountability, allowing checks and balances of various design and construction issues. Having an experienced commissioner involved in all aspects of the design and build process would have ensured smoother communication between contractors and improved project timeliness.

PROJECT USE

The building serves as the organization's central regional office and houses its statewide resource pro-

tection programs. It is also home to the Putnam Conservation Institute, an initiative formed to increase the capacity of the conservation community to protect, care for, and interpret the natural and cultural resources of Massachusetts.

The center hosts meetings, lectures, and conferences, and the facility is often rented out to independent groups and organizations. Interpretive materials in the entrance lobby describe some of the details of the various building systems and materials. With nearly 5,000 visitors in its first year alone, the center provides an incredible opportunity to educate a wide range of decision makers and consumers. Its story weaves together the promise of renewable resource use and the future of land conservation and stewardship of cultural resources.

While it is difficult to imagine that there will be a significant change in the building program and its use in the foreseeable future, the floor plan has been designed for flexibility. The offices and conference rooms that are aligned along the south wall can be increased or decreased in size within the modular grid of partitions. The interior work areas on both the first and second floors are open and flexible in plan and can be reconfigured, enlarged, or contracted as needed by future users. Currently, a number of these are configured as hotel-style workstations. This is a key feature for a statewide organization with a staff that travels. The main large conference area was designed with two movable partitions that can divide the space into three rooms of equal size or a configuration of one small and one larger meeting room.

While the initial start-up costs were higher, the gap between lower operating costs and higher start-up costs continues to widen as energy costs rise. The lower operational costs are quickly paying down that initial investment. This is particularly germane for institutions with a long-term perspective. While short-term capital expeditures are important, especially where fund raising is involved, long-term operating budgets have a much more pronounced effect on the organization's fiscal health.

TOP: The exterior massing, the siting, and the landscape plan were designed to minimize the center's impact on its surroundings. (DG)

BOTTOM: The roofs support a rack system of photovoltaic modules with modular inverters. This array generates approximately 28,000 kWh per year. (FS)

BUILDING AS EDUCATIONAL TOOL

The core mission of the Trustees of Reservations, the nation's oldest regional nonprofit conservation organization, is to protect Massachusetts's natural and historic resources for everyone to enjoy. From working farms to historic homesteads, barrier beaches to mountain vistas, the Trustees own, manage, and interpret nearly 25,000 acres on 96 reservations. In addition, the Trustees hold perpetual conservation restrictions on nearly 14,000 acres and have assisted in the protection of nearly 12,000 additional acres by partner organizations. They also own four National Historic Landmarks, a National Natural Landmark, and seven properties listed with the National Register of Historic Places.

In addition to all its other functions, the Trustees are concerned that the Doyle Conservation Center serve as an educational model of sustainable building. To that end, all of the sustainable aspects of its design are on view for the public to see. In many instances, the public's conception of sustainable design includes images of either impossibly complicated technologies or the 1970s approach of living rough. Contrary to these conceptions, the organization wanted to show by example that land and buildings can be developed in ways that use mainstream technologies in combination with creative thinking to minimize the near- and long-term impact on the environment.

The center is designed to function as a public resource and a demonstration of how the organization is managing consumption and using renewable resources for clean sources of power. There are tours and a wide variety of programs that explain the various systems in place. The features that are explained include the photovoltaic panels, the high-efficiency lighting and controls, an energy recovery "heat wheel" ventilation system, the high-performance windows and building envelope, the geothermal wells, and the carbon dioxide monitoring systems. Visitors to the center experience sustainability at work in a very user-friendly setting. The materials and systems, which are all visible and within reach, alter the perception that sustainability relies only on esoteric and costly systems.

interior cabinetry

flooring materials

Interior cabinetry is constructed utilizing products manufactured from agricultural fibers such as renewable wheat straw. Many of the flooring materials—bamboo, cork, and linoleum—are derived from renewable resources, and all carpet tiles are from recycled materials.

CONSERVATION LAW FOUNDATION CORPORATE HEADQUARTERS
BOSTON, MASSACHUSETTS

Completed:	2004
Owner:	Conservation Law Foundation
Architects:	Moskow Architects, Inc. Keith Moskow, AIA Robert Linn
Consultants:	LeMessurier Consultants—Structural Engineers Crowley Engineers—MEP Engineers Hickory Consortium—Sustainability Consultants
General Contractor:	JJ Vaccaro Inc., Phase I Gustafson Construction, Inc., Phase II
Photographer:	Greg Premru
Site:	58–64 Summer Street, Boston, MA 02110
Environment:	Urban
Program:	The project, which entails the creation of a new headquarters for the Conservation Law Foundation (CLF), was completed in two phases. The first phase included the renovation of 12,000 square feet on four floors of a nineteenth-century mercantile building. The second phase was a 9,000-square-foot expansion of foundation headquarters into an adjacent office building, and a 3,500-square-foot retrofit of CLF's existing facilities.

The "think tank," a fourth-floor conference room surrounded by open office workstations.

Square Footage:	Phase I—12,000 square feet, Phase II—9,000 square feet
Sustainable Features:	• Site selection
	• Reduced site disturbance
	• Urban redevelopment
	• Alternative transportation, public transportation access
	• Bicycle storage and changing rooms
	• Stormwater management
	• Innovative wastewater technologies
	• Water use reduction (30 percent reduction)
	• Exterior design to reduce heat islands (roof)
	• Additional commissioning
	• Ozone depletion (support early compliance with Montreal Protocol)
	• Green power (grid source, renewable energy technologies on a net zero pollution basis)
	• Light pollution reduction systems commissioning
	• Minimum energy performance, optimize energy performance (40 percent Phase II/30 percent Phase I)
	• Daylighting
Structural System:	• Existing floor, exterior wall and roof framing
	• FSC-certified wood framing infill framing
	• Recycled steel wall studs
Mechanical System:	• Closed combustion boiler with indirect storage tank for domestic hot water
	• Variable speed pumps and high efficiency fans
Materials:	• Certified sustainable wood casework and paneling
	• Low-VOC to no-VOC finishes
	• Super-efficient electric lighting with occupancy controls
	• Recycled carpet squares

The Conservation Law library stacks are integrated into the second-, third-, and fourth-floor halls. Natural light is borrowed from adjacent offices.

PROJECT DESIGN

The Conservation Law Foundation first embraced the principles of sustainable design when it renovated a building in Boston for its headquarters in 1993. At that time, the foundation and Moskow Architects focused its efforts on energy efficiency, primarily in the form of better heating equipment, efficient lighting, and the use of energy efficient equipment; the more holistic approach to sustainable building that is gaining traction today was still in its infancy. For its time, the project was a success. It also convinced the Conservation Law Foundation of the merits of building sustainably. So, when the offices were expanded a decade later into the adjacent building, the client and design team committed itself to more ambitious, far-reaching goals. Based on the foundation's active participation in all areas of the environment, its design committee members were keen to look far beyond just energy efficiency. They also wanted the new space to avoid air pollution emissions, feature better indoor air quality and more environmentally sound materials choices, waste less material during construction, conserve water, and exploit natural energy sources to improve its performance.

Given that the new space was to be located in an older building, 58 Summer Street, which had been essentially gutted and mothballed for 30 years, the project was virtually a blank slate for energy effi-

TOP: Second-floor main conference room.

BOTTOM: Workroom with hanging shelf.

ciency improvements. CLF faced an initial choice of how "green" to go. Should it use products and systems such as super-high-efficiency windows, photovoltaics, and a cogeneration plant that would take decades to pay for themselves in energy savings or should it use the project to illustrate what could be done to improve efficiency at an affordable cost? Partly because of limited funds, but mostly to produce a model that would be straightforward for other businesses to actually follow, CLF chose to install an array of readily available energy technologies and sustainable materials and systems that paid for themselves in a reasonable period.

Originally, the client and the design team planned to use the U.S. Green Building Council's LEED standard as a guide to green building, but not to attempt certification (at the time of conception, in 1998, the LEED program was in its infancy). However, the building project was put on hold during the fundraising campaign funding. By the time the design went ahead, the LEED pilot program had evolved to LEED 2.0 and the CLF pursued certification. Some of the focus areas included creating a high-performance thermal envelope, providing a very high level of indoor air quality, recycling and reducing construction waste, and creating an efficient lighting/daylighting system.

TOP: The fourth-floor conference room is flooded by natural light from above. Cork interior walls attenuate sound transmission.

BOTTOM: The reception desk is constructed of wood harvested according to the Forest Stewardship Council's standards for sustainability.

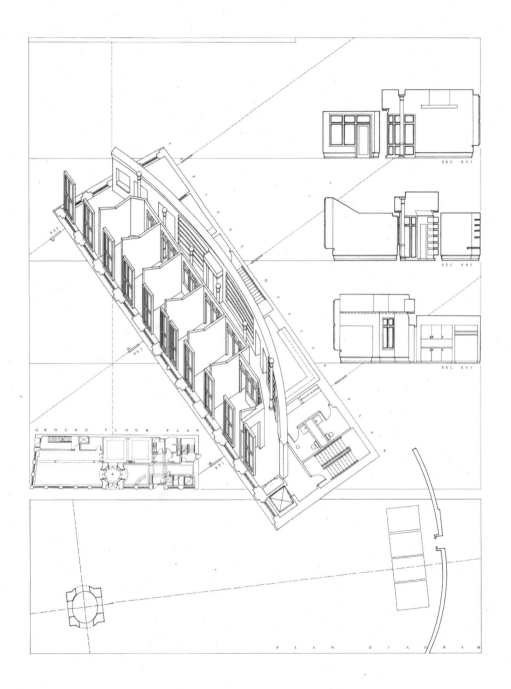

GROUND FLOOR PLAN

PLAN DIAGRAM

Isometric plan diagram.

PROJECT CONSTRUCTION

Office buildings are very different in the way they use energy than housing. Office buildings use most of their energy for lighting, heating, and cooling and, typically, this energy comes in the form of electricity—the highest-cost fuel. Consequently, our primary targets for energy savings were cooling and lighting. As an aside, appliances also offer a major opportunity for electricity savings, and a program was initiated to purchase Energy Star computers and peripherals. This was institutionalized through the creation and signature of a CLF policy to only purchase energy efficient office equipment, appliances, motors, and pumps.

Envelope energy conservation is the primary means for reducing both cooling and heating energy use. The CLF building has glazing facing primarily south and west, so the choice of low-shading-coefficient glazing cut the solar gain in summer by more than half. Because of the orientation of the glazing, the cooling load impact is high. The same glazing, with an overall U-value of .32, reduces heat loss in winter. Added wall insulation further reduces both heating and cooling loads.

Daylighting—the use of natural light to replace electric light—was another primary goal of the design. Integrating natural light and super-efficient electric lighting and controls, reduced the lighting energy use significantly. Light shelves were installed at a point one-third down from the top of the very large window openings, with the goal of reflecting light deeper into the building while shading the space nearest the window. Daylighting controls were installed in spaces at the front and back of the building that have access to large amounts of daylight. These controls reduce the power to the high-efficiency dimmable fluorescent fixtures in proportion to the available natural light.

A high level of indoor environmental quality was a key objective of the project. Each zone was supplied with fresh air with a minimum of 20 cubic feet per minute (cfm) per occupant. At the same time, low-VOC materials were selected to reduce impacts on indoor environment.

Much has recently been written about the LEED certification program, but, for the design and construction team, the new CLF headquarters put the program in a new light. By a serendipitous coincidence, there was a two-year fundraising hiatus between the completion of the building's design and the beginning of construction just as the LEED certification program was coming into being. Given CLF's commitment to the environment, once the LEED program was codified, it was an easy decision to seek certification. However, this goal was not reflected in the already completed construction documents and, therefore, had to be addressed exclusively during the construction phase. While this presented a number of challenges, it also uncovered a lot of interesting issues. First, in order to minimize the number of LEED-driven additional services, the design and construction team identified all of the LEED points that were "low-hanging fruit." What quickly became evident is that there are a lot of easy green choices. For example, it cost nothing to change the color of the roofing material from dark to light to reduce heat gain or to use drywall with a high content of

recycled gypsum. And while it required some flexibility on the part of the contractor, switching to local and regional suppliers ended up costing roughly the same as the estimates.

Second, given that access to the site was severely limited through a continuously occupied building, the LEED requirements for recycling construction debris took on special significance. Anything that could be reused on-site, such as timbers and masonry, was carefully considered.

By addressing LEED certification with a necessarily pragmatic, cost-conscious mind-set, the team realized that many of the standards were easily achieved with a fairly conventional approach.

PROJECT USE

The Conservation Law Foundation wisely decided that life cycle costs would be more important to the organization than initial costs. This allowed consideration of higher-performance envelopes, materials, systems, and equipment. Costs are a particularly important part of the equation, yet in the real world of building construction, cost estimates tend to be carried out late in the process and are initially elusive.

THIS PAGE TOP: West elevation.

THIS PAGE BOTTOM: Site plan.

OPPOSITE PAGE TOP: Fourth-floor plan.

OPPOSITE PAGE BOTTOM: Second-floor plan.

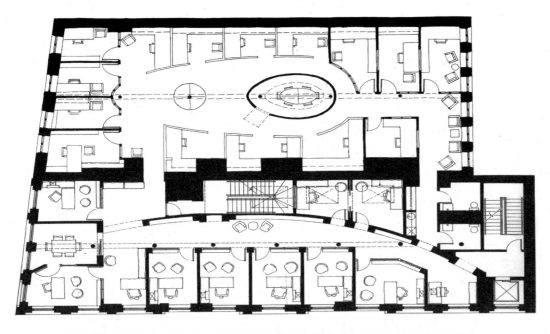

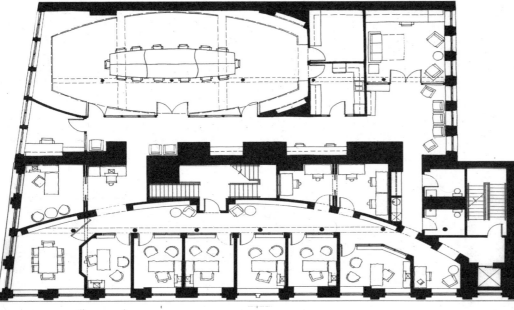

Including the higher energy/environmental specifications early in the design kept the costs to a minimum, and the cooperation of the building contractor supported the process. Appreciation of the potential economic benefits supported CLF's new view of how energy and environmental costs impact building owners. Avoidable present value of energy costs can be comparable to the building's entire capital cost and can enhance market value in proportion to the savings. Energy costs may be 15 percent or more of operating income—funds otherwise available for debt service and programs.

Energy cost estimates, based on energy use in other new office buildings and extrapolated for the new addition, show a typical annual lighting cost of around $4,706, heating and domestic hot water costs of roughly $8,726, other electric costs of $5,131, and cooling costs totaling $2,703. The comparable base case use and expected use in the new building are shown in the Annual Cost Breakdown fig-

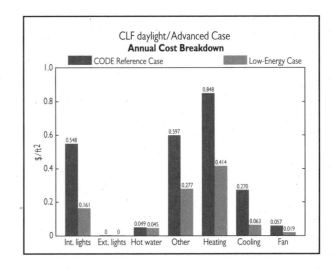

ure. Through conservation measures in each of these areas, we expect to save 59 percent of the energy costs relative to a building that just meets the Massachusetts energy code, or $12,826 per year.

Reducing or avoiding production of pollutants such as CO_2, SO_2, and NO_x has become possible in recent times as more knowledge of generation mix and production of pollutants by energy equipment is developed. The estimated reductions in CO_2 are 60 tons per year or 58 percent. For SO_2, CLF estimates a reduction of 497 lb, or 63 percent, and for NO_x a reduction of 282 lb/yr, or 61 percent. Reductions in the use of nonrenewable energy, water, and forest products will have significant benefits for the environment.

Finally, improvements in indoor environment (lighting, fresh air, comfort, health), have resulted in productivity gains among workers. Since the present costs of paying employees are tens of times the energy costs, a tiny improvement in productivity could easily outweigh the initial cost of better design. One study demonstrated that productivity gains of a mere 90 seconds per employee per day paid for the additional $1-per-square-foot cost of a well-designed building.

Building exterior.

THERMAL ENVELOPES

Given that the project was a renovation, one of the biggest challenges in terms of sustainability was how to create a tight thermal envelope. This is an especially important issue within the context of the overall building industry given the portion of construction that involves renovation and rehabilitation.

62-64 Summer St., a nineteenth-century mercantile building, features a masonry and stone exterior with large window openings and a wood and cast iron structure on the interior. The windows line the east, south, and west facade—the north wall is a party wall. As a consequence, the primary concern for the new windows was minimizing heat gain. In order to enhance the thermal performance of the walls and the roof, an approach was needed that could work with the extremely irregular surfaces of the bearing walls and compensate for the lack of thermal breaks in the roof structure.

The solutions for these two problems were fairly straightforward in terms of materials—operable, high-efficiency windows with low-E, low-solar-heat-gain glazing, blown-in cellulose for the wall cavities, and a combination of spray-on icynene and rigid insulation sheathing at the roof. The real issue, as is the case with most high-performance thermal envelopes, was making sure the systems were installed properly and testing them during the installation process. We cannot emphasize enough the importance of carefully scrutiny and testing of the envelope during installation. Following are the most significant issues that arose.

First, while there are any number of high-quality manufacturers of energy efficient windows, these products depend on the meticulous installation of the weather stripping and the thermal breaksealing of the frame to the rough opening. Given the idiosyncratic nature of renovations, the detailing for these components needs to be developed in concert with the contractor so that everyone understands the importance of proper installation.

Second, while blown-in cellulose is a relatively forgiving technology that fills in highly irregular cavities, it can easily be compromised by the trades that follow the insulation subcontractor. Once again, it is imperative that the electricians, plumbers, and HVAC contractors consider the protection of the thermal envelope as part of their scope of work as well.

Finally, in the creation of a tight thermal envelope at the roof structure, it is once again the detailing that holds the key. The material itself is fairly forgiving in its installation—it expands to fill most irregular cavities. The roof structure itself, however, must be adapted to provide thermal breaks between the structural members and the sheathing. In this instance, we added insulation board above the structure to create this break.

Perhaps the most helpful tools in assessing the quality of the thermal envelope in structures of this kind are thermal imagers and blower door tests. These should be used immediately following insulation (assuming plumbing and electric rough-in is complete) and before any other substrates or finishes are installed so that any gaps can be found and repaired while they are visible and/or easily accessible. These tests should be run again after the other trades mentioned previously are finished to ensure that the envelope has remained intact, and to give one last chance to correct omissions.

There is nothing sexy about this work, but it is the foundation upon which any energy efficient renovation rests. By establishing performance guidelines at the outset of the project and by conveying the utility and importance of these guidelines to all of the relevant subcontractors, this process can be made to work with a minimum of additional effort. But it is surprising how even fairly small problems can affect both performance and, just as important, perception of performance. This is especially true in commercial settings where employee comfort is a big issue. The irony is that the better a building performs, the higher people's expectations become. It is a good problem to have, but it is better to solve it early.

WOODS HOLE RESEARCH CENTER, GILMAN ORDWAY CAMPUS
FALMOUTH, WOODS HOLE, MASSACHUSETTS

Completed:	June 2003
Owner:	Woods Hole Research Center
Architecture:	William McDonough + Partners
	William McDonough, FAIA
	Mark Rylander, AIA, Russell Perry, Chris Hays, John Easter,
	Donna McIntire, Ana Stella, Tim Bragan, Jeff Sties, Emily Mensone,
	Carl Crawford, Maria Chao
Consultants:	Holmes and McGrath, Inc.—Civil Engineering
	Robert Silman Associates—Structural Engineering
	2RW Consulting Engineers—MEP Engineering
	Nelson Byrd—Landscape Architect
	Northern Power—Renewable Energy Consultants
	Mark Rosenbaum, PE—Energy Systems Designer & Consultant
	Clanton & Associates, Inc.—Lighting Design
General Contractor:	TR White, Inc.
Photographers:	Judy Watts Wilson (JW) Diane Quaid (DQ)
	Charles Benton (CB) Daniel Webb (DW)
	Alan Orling (AO)
Environment:	Rural/Suburban—The Woods Hole Research Center is located on the edge of a small town within a rapidly growing vacation area.

View of the center from the street showing native planting scheme. (DQ)

Program:	The facility serves as the main building for the Center. As such, it includes offices, research laboratories, and meeting spaces.
Square Footage:	7,500-square-foot renovation, 12,500-square-foot addition
Sustainable Features:	• Grid-connected, net-metered 26 kW photovoltaic (PV) arrays on top of roof and front porch
	• Space conditioned by closed-loop ground source heat pump system
	• Planned wind turbine will make building a net-energy exporter
	• All lumber is sustainably harvested
	• Operable double- and triple-glazed windows provides year-round thermal comfort
	• Web-based performance reporting (www.whrc.org)
Structural System:	• Wood with structural steel frame reinforcing
Mechanical System:	• Ground source heat pumps
	• Water to water heat exchangers and valance units
	• Water to air heat exchangers for assembly area's air-based HVAC system
Sustainable Materials:	• FSC-certified exterior Atlantic white cedar shingles and siding
	• Loewen windows with FSC-certified fir and high-performance glazing

Stairs showing daylighting scheme. (JW)

DESIGN

The adoption of an integrated, whole-building design approach enabled the client and all the consultants to work as a single design team to go further in applying sustainability as a guiding principle. The design was constrained by a desire to rehabilitate a nineteenth-century Victorian house of moderate historical interest, one of three similar and adjoining summer homes. The decision to maintain the original building reduced the possibilities for passive solar design and complicated the introduction of natural lighting into the core of the building. By renovating and expanding what is called "Hilltop," the center consolidated its scientific, policy, and administrative staffs in a single location. The central features include a two-story commons with panoramic views and a 100-person meeting facility that takes advantage of its lower level and northern exposure. A design and construction oversight team met at least weekly during the course of the project and included five members of the permanent staff of the research center. These five members remained engaged until the conclusion of the commissioning process.

The roof of the addition and the front porch support a 2,300-square-foot, 26.4-kW photovoltaic array that produces an average of 30,500 kWh of power annually. The design concept is based on the addition of a wind turbine to provide the balance of the electricity demand. The array is connected to the regional power grid, to which electricity has been flowing in times of local surplus. The heating and cooling energy is reduced through the use of a groundwater well,

35

which stays at a relatively constant temperature year-round. The water is run through modular water-to-water heat exchangers where heat is either rejected or extracted, depending on the season. The water is then returned to the standing column well.

The center relies on a variety of systems for thermal comfort, beginning with natural ventilation, enabled by operable windows in all occupied spaces. For the offices, heating and cooling are decoupled from ventilation air. Ventilation is provided to each office through enthalpy wheels, which recover heat from the exhausted air. A hydronic valence convector system provides radiant cooling and heating of the offices using significantly less energy than fan coils units would. The lab and assembly areas have separate water-to-air heat pump systems. The research center's new home optimizes the use of natural lighting for both energy efficiency and aesthetics with abundant daylight reaching all interior spaces. In the addition, the windows are clear, triple-glazed, argon-filled insulating units. In the existing building, the windows use high-performance glass but are double-glazed.

CONSTRUCTION

Due to the poor condition of the existing building, it was thoroughly gutted before reconstruction. The local climate is relatively mild in the summer

TOP: Exterior entrance showing sitework. (DW)

BOTTOM: View of addition exterior from the north. (AO)

36

months, allowing for a fair amount of passive ventilation and cooling. Winters can be cold, and the building envelope was given particular attention, including staggered stud construction with spray-on foam insulation, double- and triple-glazed windows, and careful treatment of window and door frame details. Very little land was available behind the existing structure so the use of steel in the frame was essential.

High-durability, low-maintenance, low-VOC materials, paints, and adhesives were specified throughout the center. No carpeting was used and wood for framing, window, trim, and flooring is certified by the Forest Stewardship Council. For floor framing, engineered wood products made from plantation-grown wood were used. The designers developed a simple palette: most interior materials were defined as either *silica* (glass, stone, and so on) or *cellulose* (wood) with exceptions in mechanical and electrical systems and other special parts. Other than aluminum-clad wood windows that were selected for longevity, few metal, stone, or other materials high in embodied energy were used. The building's integration of passive solar and energy conservation strategies, optimal performance, and on-site renewable power make the building 83 percent more efficient than an American Society of Heating, Refrigerating and Air-Conditioning Engineers (ASHRAE)-compliant (90.1–1989) building.

TOP: Aerial view showing photovoltaic array. (CB)

BOTTOM: View from Conference Room. (JW)

37

USE

The building represents the client's effort to show, in practical and replicable terms, how the intelligent integration of energy efficiency and renewable energy production can provide a high standard of service and comfort in an office facility in the Northeast, while simultaneously addressing the carbon-related consequences of our lifestyle. The building's systems, siting, and orientation all draw upon the natural energy flows of the sun, earth, and wind, while integrated design strategies allow the building to begin operations with dramatically reduced energy consumption—up to 60 percent below energy code. The building uses about 50 kWh/m^2/yr (16 kBtu/ft^2/yr), which is the best of its class in the Department of Energy's High Performance Buildings database. The facility is comfortable and spacious, and staff and visitors are particularly aware of the prevalence and high quality of the daylighting.

The client group made a very intelligent decision that by some counts appeared to go against conventional wisdom. Careful analysis with the design team suggested that manual rather than highly automated lighting and temperature controls would encourage the participation of the people in the building and would allow human comfort to be the determining factor for settings. Ultimately, this reinforces the role people need to play in making smart choices in using a building designed to accommodate them.

The building is an evolving teaching tool for its occupants and for others. In 2004, the Agents of Change program hosted a training session at the Woods Hole facility. Agents of Change was funded by the U.S. Department of Education Fund to better prepare students as future teachers, architects, and stewards of the built environment. The program brought two dozen educators and graduate students to the site for several days of measurement and data collection. Teams tested seven hypotheses and gathered data on each; the study areas included indoor air quality, natural ventilation, thermal comfort, acoustics, light levels, daylight, valence convector performance, and skylight contribution to daylight levels.

THIS PAGE: Conference Room from above. (AO)

OPPOSITE PAGE: Site plan.

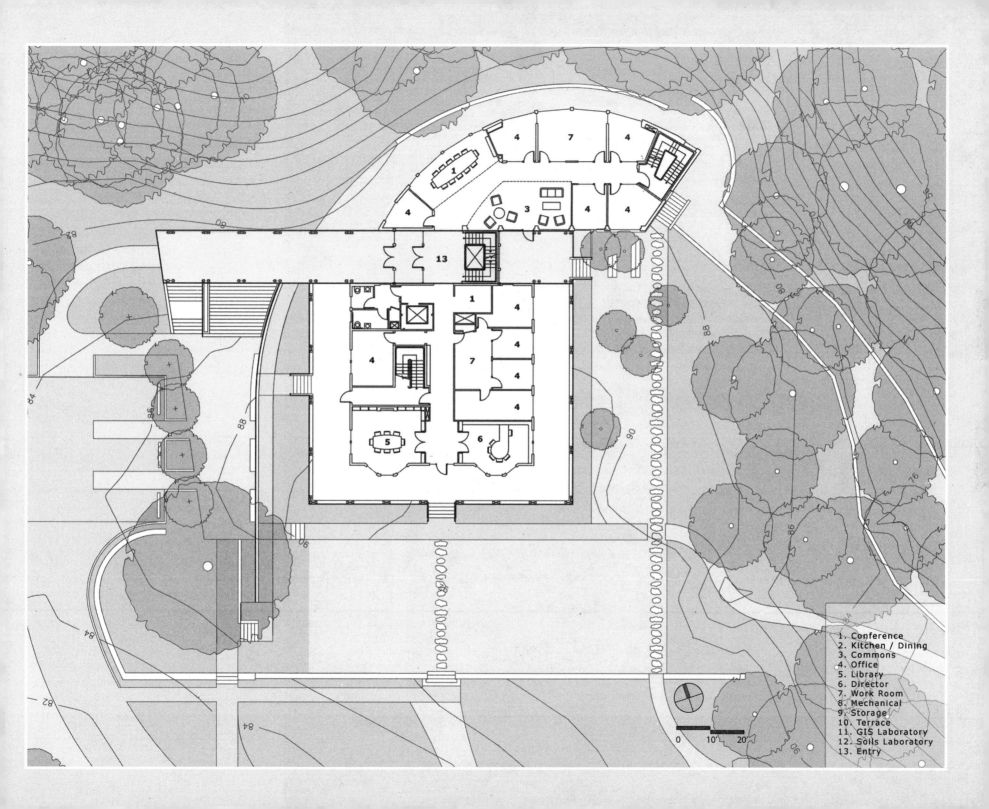

1. Conference
2. Kitchen / Dining
3. Commons
4. Office
5. Library
6. Director
7. Work Room
8. Mechanical
9. Storage
10. Terrace
11. GIS Laboratory
12. Soils Laboratory
13. Entry

0   10'   20'

View of entrance trellis. (JW)

BUILDING AS ENERGY EXPORTER

The Woods Hole Research Center is a leading scientific institution and a pioneer in the understanding of climate change and its human causes. When it came to the center's own facility, its leaders posed some challenging questions: What if a building produced more energy than it used? Or, what do buildings have to do with climate change? The center's leaders worked closely with their architects and engineers to achieve their primary goal of creating a high-performance facility—one which produces more energy than it consumes. Energy demand was calculated using Energy-10 software published by the Passive Solar Industries Council. The first year of occupancy saw a 72 percent reduction of energy use, despite the newly renovated facility being nearly twice the size of the old campus.

The building's tight envelope minimizes thermal energy outflow, and an extensive energy monitoring system records electrical production, usage, and overall system performance, which can be viewed in real time on the Woods Hole Research Center's website.

The institution currently operates using only 23 percent of the energy required to maintain a similarly sized structure. In order to curb reliance on public utilities and eventually become a net energy exporter, the research center integrates renewable energy at all stages of construction and use. As an all-electric building recognizing the distinct and often unpredictable coastal New England climate, the campus takes a hybrid approach to its renewable energy resources. A 26-kW peak (DC-rated) capacity photovoltaic solar array accounts for approximately 30 percent of the campus' energy needs (37,000 kWh of power). Eighty-eight 300-W photovoltaic panels, totaling 196 m² are connected in eleven series strings to eleven 2.5-kW SMA grid-connected intevers. The six closed-loop, ground-source heat pumps and solar thermal hot water systems take care of renewable electricity, heating and cooling, and water. A hydronic distribution system further enhances the groundwater system's effectiveness. Valence convectors provide silent radiant heating and cooling with individual zone control and greater efficiency than conventional coil fan units. Energy recovery

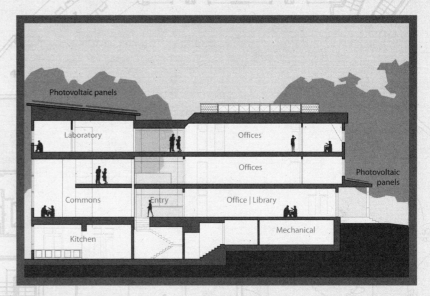

Section.

ventilators use enthalpy wheels to recapture exhaust heat and moisture, and to precondition incoming fresh air. Energy Star–rated office equipment and appliances are used whenever available, and shared use of printers and copiers is encouraged.

The center is planning to add a Northwind 100 wind turbine, funded by the Massachusetts Renewable Energy Trust. It will be located on a 40-meter monopole tower to the southeast of the building. The turbine will provide Woods Hole with over 100,000 kWh of electricity annually, potentially allowing the center to realize its goal of functioning as a net exporter of energy, meaning that the building will generate more energy than it uses. In effect this means that the facility will essentially be offsetting its neighbors' consumption to a certain degree. The integration of all these energy saving components contributes vastly to the building's overall success as a healthy and productive workplace in addition to a research institution that reflects its conservation pursuits.

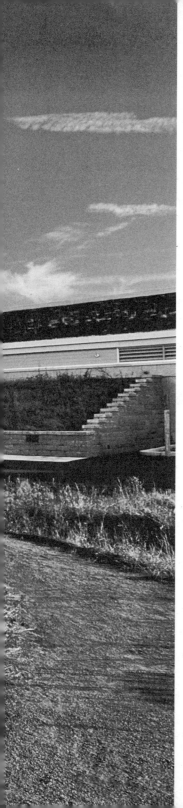

BAY EDUCATION CENTER
PROVIDENCE, RHODE ISLAND

Completed:	June 2005
Owner:	Save The Bay Inc.
Architects:	Croxton Collaborative Architects, P.C.
Consultants:	Northeast Engineers & Consultants—Civil Engineering
	Yoder + Tidwell—Structural Engineering
	Lehr Consultants International—MEP Engineering
	Andropogon Associates—Landscape Design/Site Planning
	William Armstrong Lighting Design—Lighting
	Quest Energy Group—Energy Modeling
General Contractor:	Agostini Construction
Photography:	Ruggero Vanni
Site:	The site encompasses an abandoned landfill at the southern tip of Fields Point along the shoreline of Narragansett Bay in Providence, Rhode Island.
Program:	The program includes reception, observation lobby, two classrooms, lab space, a large meeting room, and Save The Bay's administrative offices and Meeting Room. There is an adjacent boathouse with a fixed pier and dock.
Square Footage:	15,042 square feet
Sustainable Features:	• Salvaged waste concrete slabs from the site were reused as crushed concrete structural fill in the building's foundation and in reconstruction of the revetment sea wall.

Northern arrival sequence at Bay Education Center. Green roof and earthen berm allow the center to fold into the landscape.

- Salvaged granite curbing from the site was used to construct an outdoor amphitheater for the education department. Additional granite slabs from the site were also used for seating.
- Primary and overflow parking areas were constructed of pervious material to reduce stormwater runoff.
- A series of bioremediation ponds had been built on the site to clean stormwater runoff before it entered the bay. A marsh restoration project included an investigation of the multiple types of grass.
- The gas-fired heater chiller and related energy strategies produce 65 percent less NO_x and 68 percent less SO_x (acid rain) when compared to comparable mechanical systems and strategies, and produces 51 percent less CO_2 (greenhouse gas).
- The system is designed to be able to transition to renewable biofuels.
- 7,000 square feet of vegetated roof can retain approximately 5,000 gallons of water for a 24-hour period.
- Waterless urinals, dual-flush toilets, and low-flow fixtures reduce water consumption by one-third.
- The amount of electricity produced annually by the 20-kW photovoltaic rooftop array is equal to the amount of electricity required to power the building's lighting system annually.
- 100 percent shading to south glass allows for all-day, glare-free view of Narragansett Bay.

Structural System:	• Steel frame
Mechanical System:	• Gas-fired absorption heater/chiller
Materials:	• Masonry
	• Natural wood siding @ exterior
	• Masonry, glass + metal
	• Painted drywall
	• Ceramic tile, carpet @ interior

Lobby floor with laser-cut linoleum map of Narragansett Bay for children's educational uses.

PROJECT DESIGN

The Bay Education Center, the first not-for-profit educational facility located on Narragansett Bay, was conceived as a project that allows children of all economic backgrounds equal access to the beauty and enjoyment of the bay. At the same time, the center's core objective is to combine that access with an educational program to heighten awareness in all of the issues that affect the health and sustainability of this important coastal ecosystem.

In an effort to integrate the center into the surrounding landscape as much as possible, the form of the building opens up dramatically toward the water with the bulk of the fenestration on the south and east facades where views of the bay predominate. The north facade is bermed into the earth and held close to the ground. This integration of landscaping and solar orientation results in a snug, yet fully daylit building in which all occupied spaces have a view out to the bay. At the same time, the collective effect of the bermed facade, a series of connected swales, and a green roof essentially eliminates the negative effects of stormwater runoff on the bay by minimizing the amount of impervious surface.

The site, which was previously a landfill for construction debris, contained a number of raw materials that were mined as part of the design team's strategy to be resourceful and keep costs contained. Two examples of this reuse include: old concrete slabs that were crushed and utilized as structural fill below the new slab; and old granite curbing from downtown Providence that was reclaimed as seating for the outdoor amphitheater. The soil itself was repurposed as fill for the earthen berms and the entire site was capped with dredged material from the bay, once the negative effects of the landfill had been remediated.

At the outset of the project, the design team and the owners had little information on the site so the initial predesign work focused on understanding its assets, as well as the challenges it would present. The most notable issues were the scope of the revetment construction, the full EPA requirements for remediating the site, and the subsurface methane. This preliminary analysis spawned a number of creative approaches to solve difficult issues. Initially, the design team hoped to utilize the methane gas as a supplemental fuel source for the mechanical system. Unfortunately, in the final analysis, the quantities present were not sufficient. In relation to the revetment, the designers were able to use it to provide Americans with Disabilities Act (ADA) access down to the marsh restoration area. As a result, handicapped students can gain firsthand knowledge of the salt marsh habitat.

As the project moved through the design phase, both one- and two-story schemes were analyzed to address the trade-offs between creating a building with dispersed weight distribution versus one that minimized the exterior volume. Ultimately, the landform and soil-bearing capacity mandated a one-story building. The combination of that layout, however, with the revetment, allowed for the creation of a barrier-free facility with a strong connection to the site. This connection was further augmented by the creation of 14 exits at grade.

The building has a 20-kW photovoltaic array on the south roof that produces an equal percent of electricity annually as is consumed by the building's lighting system for the entire year. In addition, Save The Bay is working to partner with others to construct a wind turbine on the site. With an eye toward the future, the gas-fired mechanical system is able to shift to biofuel or other renewable fuels.

Utilizing Power DOE-2 modeling in an iterative process, the building's envelope and systems were optimized for energy efficiency and minimization of pollution contributions. The upgraded building envelope, high-performance glazing, high-efficiency lighting and controls, and gas-fired heater/chiller mechanical system work to reduce the peak energy load by a projected 73 percent while producing 65 percent less NO_x and 68 percent less SO_x when compared to comparable mechanical systems. CO_2 emissions were reduced by 51 percent. Total source energy was reduced by 47%.

PROJECT CONSTRUCTION

Materials and products were reviewed for their resource efficiency, their effect on interior air quality, and local sourcing. At the same time, these attributes were balanced with budgetary and lead time constraints. The building envelope design was developed both to maximize energy efficiency and to address the harsh coastal environment. Cedar siding and precast stone provide the tough outer skin. A high-

LEFT: Three-tiered daylighting (main, clerestory, and dormer windows) in administrative wing.

TOP RIGHT: View of the rear portico, which provides constant shade from direct sunlight on southern exposure.

BOTTOM RIGHT: View of the Bay Education Center from southeastern shore.

efficiency thermal barrier was provided through the use of blown-in insulation made from recycled materials. The Viracon high-performance glazing reduces total energy consumption by almost 10 percent while providing extensive daylighting and views throughout the building. This helps to balance the center's programmatic needs with its energy efficiency goals.

The 7,000-square-foot sloping green roof and the connected swales/rain gardens allow for a flow of stormwater equivalent to a five-year storm to be managed on-site. This serves both to help protect the bay's ecology and to provide an attractive aesthetic feature to the building. In an effort to decrease the use of water on-site, the center uses a combination of low-flow fixtures, waterless urinals, and dual-flush toilets. While these fixtures have the highest impact on the center's water usage, reducing water consumption by roughly 33 percent, they also educate the public about the value of conservation.

As is the case on the exterior, the material palette for the interiors was chosen based on sustainability and its effects on indoor air quality. Ultimately, a mix of materials was selected that includes rapidly renewable products such as linoleum and agriboard, and recycled products, such as carpeting, tile, steel, and gypsum board. All glues and adhesives are low- or no-VOC in order to support good indoor environmental quality.

PROJECT USE

Save The Bay, in its role of advocacy and stewardship of Narragansett Bay, has placed thousands of Rhode Island children out on the water for the first time,

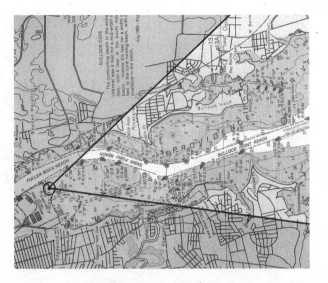

THIS PAGE TOP: Nautical map of Narragansett Bay with Bay Education Center's site location and view highlighted.

THIS PAGE BOTTOM: Site plan.

OPPOSITE PAGE TOP: Building section through administration wing.

OPPOSITE PAGE BOTTOM: North and south elevations and floor plan.

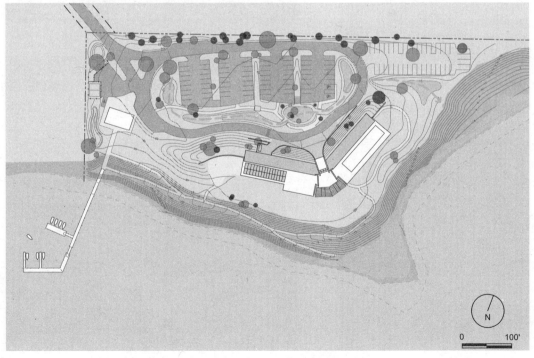

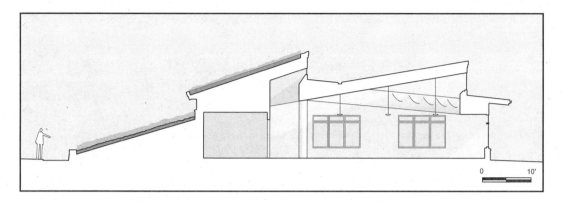

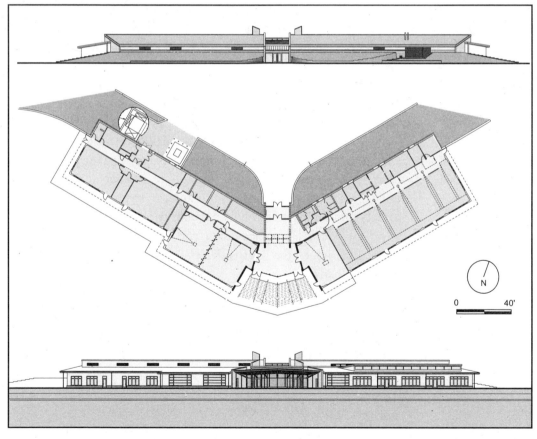

giving young citizens a powerful connection to their state's greatest natural asset. The new Bay Educational Center has given this program a permanent home on the edge of the bay supported by the classrooms, lab, outdoor amphitheater, boat house, and dock that are all located within or adjoining the south wing of the Bay Center.

The main entry is formed by an opening in the long green roof/berm at the edge of arrival parking and provides a dramatic sun-shielded panorama of Narragansett Bay as you enter. The floor, oriented exactly to the view, is a three-color, laser-cut map of the entire bay and provides visitors and students with an immediate orientation to the bay as well as a detailed graphic demonstration of the different systems of mapping: solar (or celestial) north, magnetic north, and the USGS Geodetic Mapping Grid. Students can take a visual tour of their day on the water, and visitors can appreciate the stunning scale of Rhode Island's coastline.

The North Wing houses the administrative functions of Save The Bay in a three-tiered, naturally lighted space incorporating diffuse light sails and organized as an open loft space with landscaped office planning throughout.

The lobby, the large meeting room in the South Wing, and the board room in the North Wing have proven to be very popular function spaces that are rented out for community functions and bring thousands of guests out on the bay.

Ongoing postoccupancy reviews confirm uniform enthusiasm for the daylight views and functional relationships (especially the bonus of the lobby/meeting room income) and are addressing technical challenges related to the methane extraction system and water intrusion at door sills in heavy storms.

Detail of the plantings on the "green" roof. This feature, combined with the earthen berm, allows the center to fold into the landscape.

Responding to the site's form and the desire to be set back from the coastal edge, the building maintains a uniform distance from the mean water line and forms a gateway to the bay. This positions the education wing with a direct southern view and the administration wing with a southeastern view down toward Prudence and Hog Island. The north wall is bermed up to seven feet above finish floor to insulate the wall and blend into the natural landscape. The earth insulates the north wall due to the natural stabilization of ground temperature.

The response to roof planes on most sustainable buildings is typically just to use a white rather than (heat absorbing) dark roof. However, integrating the Bay Education Center into the site as a one-story volume created several opportunities within the roof plane of the building: the green roof, clearstory windows, a photovoltaic array, and environmentally responsible roofing materials.

The 4-inch-deep vegetated roof slopes up toward the coastal edge, continuing the sloped plane of the north berm and creating a unique visual experience. This green roof will retain approximately 5,000 gallons of water for a 24-hour period, reducing the stormwater demands of the limited areas on the site. In addition, it insulates the building from solar heat gain in the summer to reduce operating costs, protects the roofing membrane from ultraviolet (UV) degradation to extend the roof's life, improves air and water quality, absorbs solar radiation to reduce the heat island effect, and provides green space and wildlife habitats.

The recycled steel standing seam roof, located over the north lobby, has a 50-year life span and doesn't pollute rainwater runoff from the roof. Traditional asphalt shingle roofs, and other petrochemical-based products, have hydrocarbon particulates that are picked up by rainwater. The remainder of the exposed roof is a rubber ethylene propylene diene monomer (EPDM) roof assembly, also more environmentally friendly than the standard asphalt installation. In addition, it is Energy Star–rated to reduce solar heat gain and reduce the heat island effect.

LEED: TO CERTIFY OR NOT, A CLIENT'S CHOICE

While the Bay Education Center did not apply for the U.S. Green Building Council (USGBC)'s LEED certification to validate its sustainable characteristics, the design of the project reflects the goal of the program to promote high-performance sustainable design. At the outset of the project in 2001, discussions were held with Save The Bay regarding LEED certification. At that time the USGBC had released the first version of the certification program, and there were only a handful of certified projects in the country (the Chesapeake Bay Foundation's Merrill Environmental Center—the first Platinum certification—was completed in 2000). The design team estimates that the Bay Education Center could have received a Gold rating if the project had been certified.

The decision to not apply for certification was based upon two primary issues, the foremost being the site-driven nature of the project and the generally building-centric focus of the LEED program. The second is the stringent requirement for the appropriate use of funds for a nonprofit organization. While the revetment restoration, brownfield encapsulation, methane catchment system, stormwater design, and dock installation represented approximately 40 percent of the project costs, these efforts would have been applicable only to approximately 6 percent of the allowable points. At the beginning of the project, it was well known that the certification process was expensive, lengthy, and somewhat unknown territory because so few projects had completed the process. This translated into an expensive endeavor for the client to pay additional fees to each member of the design team and the contractor's team in order to develop and compile the certification submission of design drawings, subcontractor submittals, and additional testing. Instead, these resources were utilized in the building's construction and site development.

Further complicating the project was an already tight budget for an ambitious project with many brownfield site issues to address. In 2000, there was no funding available to nonprofits that wanted to obtain certification (currently, the Kresge Foundation offers grants for

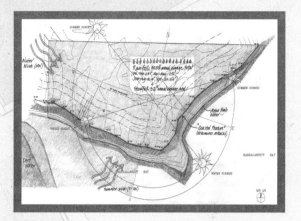

Environmental considerations for site of Bay Education Center, including solar traverse, precipitation, and seasonal winds.

both environmental upgrades and a portion of the cost of the USGBC certification process). Therefore, further value engineering would have been required to allocate funds for the certification process which would have limited Save The Bay's ability to meet its mission with this project.

More recently, many organizations have started to question the inflexibility of the LEED programs in addressing unique local and site issues. While few people argue that LEED has led the market transformation to green buildings, and the point-based system, with its simplification of issues, has spurred greater access and utilization within the building industry, it was felt by Save The Bay that the certification process would be costly within a very limited budget and not fully responsive to the unique issues of a project site and climate.

POCONO ENVIRONMENTAL EDUCATION/VISITOR ACTIVITY CENTER

DINGMANS FERRY, PENNSYLVANIA

Completed:	2005
Owner:	National Park Service/Pocono Environmental Education Center
Architects:	Bohlin Cywinski Jackson Peter Q. Bohlin, FAIA—Principal for Design Allen H. Kachel, AIA LEED AP—Project Manager Wayne Stitt, AIA—Project Architect Craig Sachse, Brent Stebbins
Consultants:	McGoey, Hauser & Edsall, P.C.—Civil Engineers E.D. Pons and Associates—Structural Engineers Strunk-Albert Engineering—MEP Engineers
General Contractor:	Pride Enterprises, Inc., Norristown, Pennsylvania
Photographers:	Thomas E. Solon, AIA, Bushkill, Pennsylvania (TS) Nic Lehoux, Vancouver, British Columbia (NL) PEEC
Site:	The site is an open clearing located on the client's campus, which is predominantly native forest containing mixed oaks, various conifers, and a well-developed understory. The environmental education center is located within the Delaware Water Gap National Recreation Area, operated by the National Park Service.

View looking east, showing the basic structural system. (NL)

Environment:	Rural—the Environmental Education/Visitor Activity Center is set within a protected forest.
Program:	The building is a gathering space for dining, meetings, lectures, and other environmental learning activities. The design is a layered solution in which visitors pass through the forest, cross a wetland, enter the building through an opening in the dark north wall, and cross through a bar of service spaces into the bright, sunlit main room. The great south-facing shed is designed to take full advantage of the sun's warmth, cool mountain breezes, abundant natural light, and views of the forest to the south. In addition to its function as the main gathering, dining, and meeting space for visitors attending the programs at the environmental center, the Environmental Education/Visitor Activity Center serves as meeting place, conference center, and public hall for community and environmental groups in the region, generating revenue for the environmental center and heightening local community awareness of the center's mission and the responsibility we all share in protecting our environment.
Square Footage:	7,750 square feet
Sustainable Features:	• Building placement to optimize passive solar and minimize site disturbance • Passive solar cooling and ventilation • Indigenous low-maintenance landscaping • Extensive use of daylighting augmented with fluorescent motion sensor–controlled lighting • Supplemental radiant heat with a concrete floor slab thermal flywheel • Low maintenance, long-lived materials • Extensive use of reused, recycled, or recyclable materials • Extensive use of low- or zero-VOC products and finishes • Extensive use of engineered wood products • Extensive use of DOE-2 energy modeling

Glue-laminated Douglas fir and exposed steel trusses create a simple, yet structurally sound framework. (NL)

Structural System:

- Frame: Douglas fir glue-laminated timber beams/columns and glue-laminated timber/steel trusses, wood stud bearing wall, cast-in-place concrete frame
- Floor: thermal mass cast-in-place concrete slab with integral color
- Low roof: plywood roof deck on wood I-joists
- High roof: stress-skin insulated plywood panels with Douglas fir finish face
- Partitions: wood stud with gypsum wall board (GWB), ground face concrete masonry unit (CMU)

Mechanical System:

- Passive solar heat and natural ventilation/daylighting
- Backup systems include hydronic radiant heat incorporated into floor slab and ceiling fans to assist natural ventilation
- Kitchen areas—ducted makeup air and exhaust system with unit heaters where required

Materials:

- Rubber shingles fabricated from reclaimed passenger tires
- Cement board siding
- Modified bituminous roofing
- Thermally broken windows/curtain wall with low-E argon-filled insulated glass with thermally broken spacer
- Silicate-based mineral paint (cement board)
- Water-based stain (glu-lams, plywood, stress-skin panels)
- Water-based stain (glu-lams, plywood, stress-skin panels)
- Latex paint (GWB walls)
- Exposed concrete frame & ground face CMU (lobby and main activity area)
- Slate wall panels (lobby)
- Recycled rubber flooring (lobby)
- Recycled content porcelain tile (kitchen and serving area)
- Integrally colored concrete slab (main activity area)
- Solid core select white maple doors, stile and rail-glazed wood entrance doors
- Douglas fir framing for slate panel supports

PROJECT DESIGN

By establishing a sustainable strategy for the design and construction of the Environmental Education/Visitor Activity Center at the beginning, the design team developed a shared set of values with the client that promoted decision testing throughout the design process. The approach provided a common framework for evaluating design and materials choices as the project developed. Consequently education became a part of the project's commitment to sustainability from the outset.

The highly collaborative design process engaged both staff and visitors, and this interactive process resulted in a building that gives its users a palpable sense of ownership. Hands-on activities, such as nature drawings done by local school children, helped to educate users about the design process. Some of the drawings were later etched into the building's block wall. Seeing their own work incorporated into the final design gave the children a tangible reminder of their participation in the project.

During the early stages of the project, the design process focused on evaluating the specific needs of the client, as well as the campus and existing facilities. Predesign studies explored options that would meet the client's limited resources, renovating and/or adding to the existing facilities. These studies also examined the potential impact of each design solution on the surrounding natural environment, local waterways, and wildlife. Although many of the options explored met the client's minimum program, they all had some negative impacts on other aspects of the client's operations. Fortunately, these studies spurred the client's governmental sponsor to appropriate funding for a freestanding design that met the client's program while eliminating any negative operational impacts.

In addition to providing a high degree of access to all of the user groups, the design process utilized a series of rigorous analytical and technical studies to test the design's appropriateness and to validate and fine-tune the environmental strategies. The environmental assessment and DOE-2 energy model were critical in evaluating and adjusting the emerging design. Studies included "right-sizing" the solution to optimize efficiency and minimize square footage.

The process also involved intensive research to ensure selection of the most appropriate materials, as well as their most cost-effective and efficient use. One study developed several alternative roof structures. Long span systems were evaluated to determine the most cost-effective solution to provide a column-free main gathering space. The solution—a stress skin panel roof diaphragm supported on engineered glue-laminated timbers—maximized the efficiency of each product. The design of the combination glue-laminated timber/steel trusses greatly reduced the cross section of the wood member

TOP: Manual devices rather than automated systems supplement natural approaches in the design of a mechanical system. Users make direct energy choices in this one-to-one connection with nature and its built environment. (NL)

BOTTOM LEFT: North facade. (NL)

BOTTOM RIGHT: View of the center's south facade at night. (NL)

through the addition of the steel trusswork, maximizing material efficiency while creating a unique aesthetic for the structural system. In retrospect, one of the most difficult balances to maintain during the design process was to keep the many highly technical aspects of the project accessible to the decision makers and the user groups.

PROJECT CONSTRUCTION

The construction process for the Environmental Education/Visitor Activity Center involved several unique environmental challenges, including the examination of local wildlife cycles in order to best protect the habitats of various species during construction. In particular, the Indiana fruit bat migrates seasonally to the region, nesting under tree bark, including areas surrounding the project. Time periods for tree felling were carefully restricted during construction in order to respect the bat's habitat.

During construction, another teaching opportunity was incorporated into the building. The process of transforming discarded automobile tires into shingles for the building's north wall offered an opportunity to enlighten visitors on environmental responsibility. After tires were collected from the local river, roadsides, and other local sources, they were cut on-site into shingles, reinforcing green decision making for visitors watching the process firsthand.

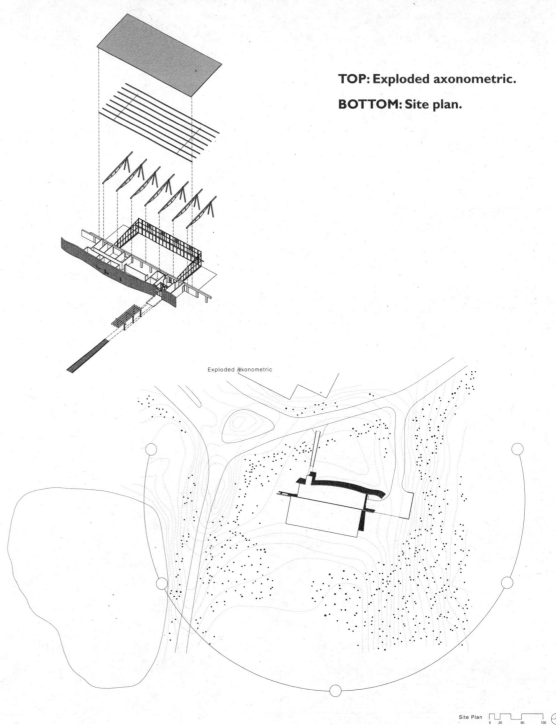

TOP: Exploded axonometric.

BOTTOM: Site plan.

Exploded Axonometric

Site Plan   0   20   60   100

PROJECT USE

Since it opened, the Environmental Education/Visitor Activity Center has proven to be almost maintenance free. The surrounding landscape developed as part of the project requires no upkeep. The rubber tire shingles, cement board siding painted with silicate mineral paint, and natural concrete block wall require no exterior maintenance. Inside, carefully selected materials make for an environment that requires little in the way of cleaning or maintenance. Natural daylighting, natural ventilation, and passive solar heat have proven effective in day-to-day use during much of the facility's operating season. Under most conditions, supplemental lighting and mechanical systems are not used.

Finally, the building's role as teaching tool has made it an integral part of the culture of the client's campus. The tire-shingled north wall teaches visitors about waste management and reuse. Children learn about energy conservation and the forces of nature by operating the window ventilators on the east, west, and south walls. The etched nature images in the block wall present a learning experience for children, offering opportunities for scavenger hunts to find animal tracks, leaf patterns, and local wildlife.

Legend

1	Vestibule
2	Entrance Foyer
3	Restroom
4	Storage
5	Main Activity Space
6	Serving Area
7	Kitchen
8	Office
9	Locker room
10	Dishwashing
11	Dry storage
12	Walk-in cooler
13	Mechanical
14	Porch

Floor Plan   0 4   12   20

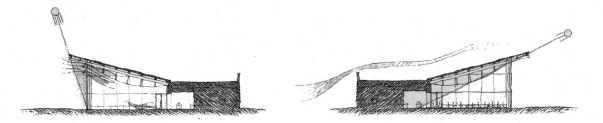

TOP: Floor plan.

BOTTOM LEFT: Transverse section looking west.

BOTTOM RIGHT: Section at winter solstice.

Orientation of a south roof overhang and large east and west porches maximizes passive solar heat gain while eliminating exposure to harsh winter winds. (TS)

The orientation and massing of the Environmental Education/Visitor Activity Center maximize the site's passive solar and natural ventilation potential using simple strategies with enormous benefits. The long south face maximizes solar gain in winter months and the floor slab of the main space serves as a heat sink to store solar energy. Conversely, the building's north side shields against winter winds. The tilted main roof aids both of these functions, maximizing solar radiation and light to the south while deflecting north winds. Light-colored roof covering minimizes the heat island effect on the surrounding environment.

Cool air from shaded porches to the east and west and warmer air, exhausted through high windows on the south face, optimize natural ventilation. The porches and south roof overhang also shield the building from direct summer sun. The sloped main roof moves warm interior air to the high exhaust windows, while the Venturi effect aids ventilation as wind moves over the roof outside. To increase natural ventilation during extreme conditions, the south face of the main space contains large sliding doors that can be opened to maximize ventilation.

Site Plan

CREATIVE USE OF MATERIALS (RUBBER TIRE SHINGLES)

ABOVE: Harvested by local volunteers, discarded automobile tires await their destiny. Local volunteers harvest discarded tires to be used for the canter's exterior sheathing. (PEEC)

LEFT: Detail of tire "shingles"—from trash to building material. (NL)

Materials incorporated into the Environmental Education/Visitor Activity Center, such as recycled tire cladding, were selected for their potential visual impact as examples of environmental design, reinforcing the building's role as a teaching tool. The north wall's unique tire cladding enabled the construction process itself to serve as a learning opportunity. Local volunteers harvested discarded automobile tires from the nearby river, roadsides, parks, and other local sources. Specialists on-site cut the tires that once littered the area into shingles, sending a powerful message to both visitors and staff who watched the tires' transformation from waste product to building material. The north wall continues to pose a visible challenge to visitors to embrace environmental responsibility.

CHESAPEAKE BAY FOUNDATION, PHILIP MERRILL ENVIRONMENTAL CENTER

ANNAPOLIS, MARYLAND

Completed:	November, 2000
Owner:	The Chesapeake Bay Foundation
Architects:	SmithGroup, Inc. Greg Mella, AIA, LEED AP, Project Architect J. Harrison Architect—LEED Coordinator
Consultants:	Greenman-Pedersen, Inc.—Civil Engineering Shemro Engineering, Inc.—Structural Engineers SmithGroup, Inc.—MEP Engineers Synthesis★—Program Manager Karene Motivans—Landscape Architects
General Contractor:	The Clark Construction Group, Inc.
Photographer:	Prakash Patel
Site:	The site is situated on 31 acres of Chesapeake Bay shoreline, located about 15 minutes southeast of Annapolis, Maryland. Previous to CBF's purchase, the site served as a community pool and inn and was planned for significant development, creating a negative impact to the bay.
Environment:	Suburban—the site is within a designated Maryland's Smart Growth zone.

Exterior view from the southwest—parallel strand timber beams, selected for their recycled content, originate from new growth trees, are FSC harvested, and sustainably regenerated.

Program:

The project consolidates a 90-person environmental staff from four dispersed buildings into a single 32,000-square-foot facility. It is designed to support and explicitly assert the principles of the Chesapeake Bay Foundation's mission—collaboration in achieving a sustainable relationship with the Chesapeake Bay. The interior of the headquarters features open office workstations for all staff members (including the president), dispersed meeting rooms throughout, a 40-person conference center, and a dining room and kitchen (lunch is catered every day).

Square Footage: 32,000 square feet

Sustainable Features:

- Reduced impervious surfaces
- Bioretention filters to treat all stormwater runoff
- Xeriscaping and drought tolerant native vegetation landscaping
- Rainwater collection, and reuse—rainwater from the building's roofs is collected and stored in exposed collection cisterns
- Waterless toilets and urinals using the composting process to convert waste to fertilizer used on-site
- Mixed-mode natural ventilation system—indoor/outdoor temperature and humidity sensors notify occupants when conditions are optimal for natural ventilation; employees manually open windows and the mechanical system turns off.
- 2-kW photovoltaic array provides electricity for lighting and equipment.
- Passive solar design—the building harnesses winter sun for heating, but fixed wooden louvers along the south facing porch shield the summer sun from overheating the interior.
- Solar domestic hot water system
- Geothermal heat pump cooling and heating system
- Desiccant dehumidification system
- Demand-controlled ventilation system with CO_2 sensors to control the amount of outside air introduced to the building based on building occupancy
- Daylighting with dimmable lighting and daylight sensors
- Occupancy sensors and controls
- Computerized energy management system used to control systems and monitor energy usage

- Efficient envelope insulation—low-E-coated insulated glass filled with argon between the lites, R-25 wall insulation, and R-32 roof insulation
- Parallel strand timber structural system
- Structurally insulated panels (SIPs) roof and wall enclosure
- High recycled content materials including galvanized steel siding and roofing, reclaimed concrete, acoustic ceiling tiles, interior fabrics, and rubber flooring
- Rapidly renewable finishes include bamboo and cork
- Salvaged wood exterior sun shades and exterior wood trim.
- Certified wood/ACQ treated wood—all wood used on the job is certified as sustainable by the Forest Stewardship Council
- Over 20 percent of the materials used in the building were manufactured within 300 miles of the building site
- Carbon monoxide and VOC sensors to monitor indoor air quality

Structural System:
- Parallel strand timber beams and posts with roof and wall enclosure using structurally insulated panels (SIPs).

Mechanical System:
- Ground source (geothermal) heat pump system.

Materials:
- Ground-face CMU block
- Galvalume steel siding and standing seam roofing
- Stained cement fiber board
- Salvaged wood trim
- Cork, bamboo flooring, and linoleum flooring
- Exposed medium-density fiberboard millwork
- Sealed SIP panels left exposed create wall and ceiling finishes
- Whenever possible, materials left unpainted, conserving resources and diminishing pollutants

TOP: Organized in four quadrants, two on each floor, the headquarters' double height lobby and exhibit space functions as an interactive node for both employees and visitors alike.

BOTTOM: Views of the bay from every work area, made possible by the building orientation and an open floor plan, encourages team interaction yet appropriate separation for individual and group work.

PROJECT DESIGN

The Philip Merrill Environmental Center used the Leadership in Environmental and Energy Design (LEED) rating system of the U.S. Green Building Council as a guiding framework for design. The council, an organization that measures sustainability in the building industry, awarded the center its highest level of certification—Platinum. It was the first building in the world to achieve this rating. The design of the headquarters set out to lead by example, hoping the Merrill Center wouldn't stay the only Platinum for long. The Center has become a destination: business owners, government leaders, contractors, architects, engineers, and the general public have come to the headquarters to learn how to build green. The wide embrace of sustainability within the building industry over the last five years suggests the goal of leading by example has been met.

The design began with the development of a master plan that set aside all but 4.5 acres of the 31-acre site under a conservation easement. This allows the majority of the site to permanently remain undeveloped. As a part of the building process, the site was restored to the representative ecosystems found within the bay's watershed including woodlands, wetlands, and even an oyster reef. To minimize site disruptions, the building and parking lot were sited over the footprint of the former pool house.

The building design connects the foundation to the bay with a strikingly simple form. It does not try to compete with a rich site, but neither does it spread out and sink down apologetically. It is composed of two shed/roof structures oriented to the south that harness views of the bay and its breezes, as well as the sun's energy for light and heat. One shed, which presents its broad face to the bay, is long and narrow. It houses the reception area, offices, and support functions. Another shed structure, which is pulled away from the south bay side, is equal in height, but has a much smaller, entirely square footprint. It serves as the conference space with an attached staff lunchroom and kitchen. The two structures sit gracefully on slender pilings that hover above the landscape. The two are connected by a large deck.

Occupants can park under the building, thus minimizing the site disruptions that are typically associated with parking. By expressing the conference space as a separate structure, the consistency of the longer, primary mass is relieved, and the resulting T-shaped building creates a degree of enclosure for the deck while focusing views to the bay. The north elevation integrates three huge rainwater storage tanks into its composition. Formally these provide relief to the expanse of the long north side of the building, marking an entry, but they also function as signage, communicating to visitors the idea that this is not a conventional office building but one that uses alternative technologies.

The building interior is organized into four quadrants, two on each floor, each separated by the central lobby and exhibit space. Each quadrant accommodates a different department, whose layout of open workstations is unique to that department. Closed offices were minimized to promote an open exchange of ideas. Open workstations replace closed offices, allowing every employee views of the bay, as well as enabling sustainable strategies such as daylighting and natural ventilation. Meeting rooms and other shared spaces within each department provide opportunities for private dialogues.

TOP: Detail of north entrance and rainwater cisterns. The use of rainwater results in 92 percent less potable water usage than in a standard office building.

CENTER: Headquarters view across the Chesapeake Bay from the west, showing entry and rainwater cisterns.

BOTTOM: Southwest view from the bay, showing the structural system.

The interior continues the theme started on the exterior of exposing many of the building's environmental innovations. Where possible, the materials are left unfinished, and ductwork is often exposed. This minimizes the use and consumption of finish materials. Much of the time the sense of completeness is provided by choice of material and composition, rather than by conventional finish. Nonetheless, where sustainable product such as cork and engineered woods are used, they are able to achieve the same qualities of warmth and familiarity as their conventional hardwood counterpoints.

On balance, the effect of the overall design of the building is to reinforce all aspects of its sustainable architecture. The clear benefits of its various systems such as daylighting and natural ventilation are object lessons to both the users and to a lesser degree to visitors. In addition, the users are encouraged to participate actively in the building's operation to optimize its performance, and to think of it more as a dynamic system than a static backdrop.

PROJECT CONSTRUCTION

The construction of the building incorporated a cradle-to-cradle rather than cradle-to-grave philosophy. This philosophy requires consideration of all materials not only for what they are made of, but also what they can be made into at the end of their useful lives. Materials were selected for recycled content (galvanized siding made from cans, cars, and guns, for example). Likewise, materials from renewable or regenerable resources were incorporated (cork flooring comes from the bark of the cork oak tree, which can

be harvested without killing the tree and regenerates in seven to nine years). All wood was either certified by U.S. Forestry Stewardship Council as coming from sustainably harvested forests or was from renewable resources (like the main foyer's bamboo flooring that is harvested from plants that regrow in approximately three years).

Existing structures on the site were deconstructed rather than demolished, and all materials were auctioned, salvaged, or recycled. The existing foundations were chipped and used as road base. Seven loads of chipped concrete were hauled offsite to be reused. The contractor used a construction recycling plan during construction of the building to minimize contribution to landfills. All cardboard, metals, concrete, concrete masonry units (CMU), asphalt, and land-clearing debris were recycled. Erosion control measures were rigorously enforced to ensure construction sedimentation and erosion did not directly impact the bay. An air quality management plan was used during the project's construction to minimize dust and debris from collecting inside the mechanical system and to prevent VOCs from being absorbed in porous building finishes.

Construction administration was performed by the team architect already familiar with the design and project goals. The contractor had limited experience with the building systems and the green process, and the project might have benefited from increased contractor and subcontractor education.

The building was commissioned in 2001 when it opened, and several small glitches in the mechanical controls were identified. For instance, the perimeter hydronic heating had not been tied into the mixed-mode natural ventilation controls as the design had dictated. As a result, the finned tube radiators

were turning on when the operable windows were opened. The problem was easily solved by adjusting controls sequences. Beyond formal commissioning, the center's facility manager has fine-tuned the building systems to be as efficient as possible without sacrificing comfort.

PROJECT USE

Since moving into the Merrill Center in 2000, CBF has done extensive work with the National Renewable Energy Laboratory (NREL) of the Department of Energy National Laboratory. NREL monitored the building's energy and water performance from November 2001 to November 2002. Annual energy usage was measured to be 39.9 kBtu/square foot/year, inclusive of plug loads and miscellaneous loads like exterior lighting and elevators. This is 59.0 percent less than typical office buildings based on 1995 data collected by the Energy Information Administration. Through NREL's analysis, CBF learned their plug loads were higher than what had been anticipated, so they went back to verify that all possible plug-ins, including soda machines, were on motion sensors, and that all office equipment purchased was Energy Star–rated. The center clearly leads by example, and the research done postoperation will be helpful for planning future high-performing commercial building designs.

NREL's monitoring also looked at the building's water consumption. Total water usage for one year was 39,937 gallons, of which 33,372 gallons (83.5 percent) was provided by way of rainwater harvest-

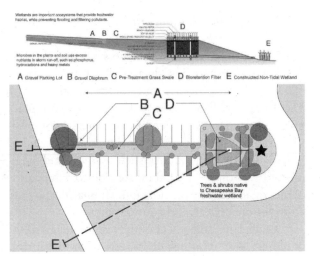

TOP: Bioretention plan.

BOTTOM: First-floor plan.

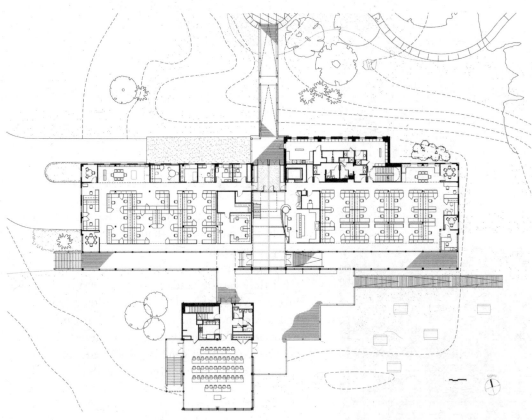

TOP: Wind diagram.

BOTTOM: Building section.

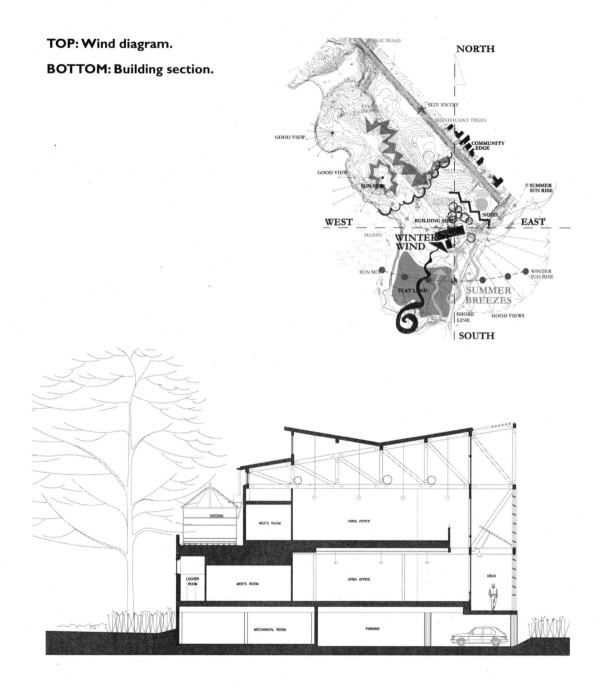

ing and reuse. The balance of water usage, 6,565 gallons (16.5 percent), was supplied by the on-site well. Total water usage at CBF averaged 1.25 gallons/square foot/year. According to BOCA Plumbing Code, a conventional office building uses 12.66 gallons/square foot/year. Thus, CBF uses approximately 10 percent of the water of a conventional office building. Such a significant reduction is attributed to composting toilets and rainwater harvesting and reuse at lavatories, clothes washer, and mop sinks. CBF reports that the composting toilets work better than expected. While CBF staff doesn't think twice about them, composting toilets are a real interest for visitors. Maintenance is minimal and compost is applied to grounds around the facility. For a 30-acre site that has been restored to native ecosystems, CBF could use all of the compost it can get.

While conserving water and energy, the Merrill Center would also have to be an effective and inspiring workplace for the 90-plus staff who work everyday inside. A study conducted by the Center for the Built Environment at the University of California, Berkeley, surveyed 25,000 occupants of 150 buildings to question users' satisfaction regarding air quality, comfort, acoustics, and lighting. Of the 150 buildings rated, the Philip Merrill Environmental Center received the second highest overall satisfaction score. Mary Tod Winchester, CBF's vice president of administration, states, "The facility is a major recruitment tool. We have a much higher level of job applicants and more applicants per job than before we moved here."

NATURAL VENTILATION

A goal for the design of the Merrill Center was to provide passive cooling through natural ventilation for a portion of the year. While this is feasible in smaller projects or in more moderate climates, naturally ventilating an office building in the hot, humid mid-Atlantic climate can be a challenge. By gathering climate data from Thomas Point lighthouse, located just off the shore from the Merrill Center, the SmithGroup estimated that the climate could support natural ventilation for approximately 9 percent of the year—when outdoor conditions were between 68° and 77°F (20° and 25°C) and 20 to 70 percent relative humidity.

The building was oriented to take advantage of cool spring and fall breezes coming off of the bay. Awning windows in the south facade were located low to catch breezes from the bay. High awning windows along the north elevation and in each of the dormers were located to maximize stack and cross ventilation. Window locations and sizes were dictated by research into the wind effects and flow patterns throughout the building. Running continuously along the inside of the south facade, a 5-foot-wide slot between the first and second floors was added to increase air circulation throughout the space.

The outside temperature and humidity is constantly monitored by the building's energy management system, and when it is determined that outdoor conditions are suitable for natural ventilation, the dormer windows will open automatically, a green light will turn on throughout the building signaling users to open the operable windows, and the mechanical system will shut down. Operable windows are ganged together to minimize the effort of opening the many windows that span the facade. This approach might not be appropriate for every type of client, but the staff of CBF is more than willing to actively

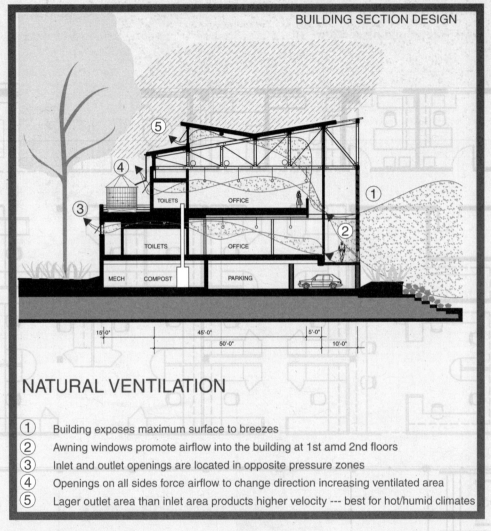

BUILDING SECTION DESIGN

NATURAL VENTILATION

① Building exposes maximum surface to breezes

② Awning windows promote airflow into the building at 1st amd 2nd floors

③ Inlet and outlet openings are located in opposite pressure zones

④ Openings on all sides force airflow to change direction increasing ventilated area

⑤ Lager outlet area than inlet area products higher velocity --- best for hot/humid climates

Natural ventilation.

engage in the operation and performance of the building. By replacing costly motorized operators, this sweat equity does dramatically reduce the cost of the mixed-mode natural ventilation system. This combina-

tion of high-tech and low-tech solutions is found throughout the Merrill Center. With very few exceptions, the Merrill Center used strategies like natural ventilation, composting toilets, geothermal cooling, and daylighting, which have been used successfully before in smaller buildings. What is most unique about the Merrill Center is the breadth of strategies used and the combined effect to reduce resource consumption in a larger scaled design. By polling staff, CBF was able to expand the temperature range where the building could be cooled using natural ventilation, while maintaining the comfort of the building occupants. The systems in the building were interactive enough to accommodate this adjustment.

Roger Chang, a graduate student at the Massachusetts Institute of Technology, Cambridge, studied the center as part of his master's thesis and reported his findings in "Case Studies of Naturally Ventilated Commercial Buildings in the United States" (2002). Chang found this estimate to be conservative and, through the use of data loggers, discovered that natural ventilation was used for 34 percent of weekday working hours during a much larger and cooler range of outdoor temperatures. Because the monitoring systems will only trigger natural ventilation during times when humidity levels do not exceed 70 percent, there are no impacts on materials that result from excess humidity indoors. Based on detailed thermal comfort surveys, Chang learned the center's occupants generally favored the use of natural ventilation compared with mechanical conditioning. The survey results also show that occupant thermal-comfort expectations differed between natural ventilation mode and mechanical air-conditioning, a fact that could partially explain the greater than anticipated use of natural ventilation at the center. A finding like that can expand the viability of natural ventilation in climates that were previously thought to be poor candidates for passive cooling.

Interior lobby from the ground floor—daylighting, natural ventilation, and use of low-VOC furnishings and finishes encourage a positive work environment.

KRESGE FOUNDATION HEADQUARTERS
TROY, MICHIGAN

Completed:	2006
Owner:	The Kresge Foundation
Architects:	Valerio Dewalt Train Associates, Inc.—Design Architect
	Farr and Associates—Associate Architects
Consultants:	Robert Darvas Associates—Structural Engineers
	ARUP—MEP Engineers
	Searl and Associates—Interior Design
	Conservation Design Forum—Landscape Architects
	Lighting Design Alliance—Lighting Design
General Contractor:	JM Olson
Photographer:	Barbara Karant (BK)
	Justin Maconochie (JM)
Site:	Three-acre historic farmstead that includes the original farmhouse, a barn, and several smaller outbuildings.
Environment:	Suburban—sited along Big Beaver Road in suburban Troy, Michigan, the Kresge Foundation Headquarters is a three-acre island bracketed by the two iconic surfaces of the American suburb—the lawn and its alter ego, the parking lot.

Gabion walls—heavy-duty wire filled with recycled demolition rubble, then capped with native crushed granite, form retaining walls. (BK)

Program:	Located on a preserved suburban farmstead, the building is designed to achieve three principal objectives: preserve and reuse the existing farm structures, some as old as 150 years; integrate the new building seamlessly with the old; and demonstrate sustainable building strategies by qualifying for a high LEED rating.
Square Footage:	19,550 square feet—new construction 6,562 square feet—renovation/remodeling
Sustainable Features:	• Closed-loop geothermal heating & cooling system • Passive solar design • Daylight harvesting • Comprehensive stormwater management including pervious pavement, bioswales, constructed wetlands, and cisterns • Intensive green roof • Underfloor air distribution • Native and adaptive vegetation
Structural System:	• Cast-in-place spread footings with steel structure
Mechanical System:	• Closed-loop geothermal system with heat pumps • Underfloor air distribution used throughout
Materials:	• Clear anodized aluminum rainscreen system with a custom-abraded surface • Green roof • Low-E glazing and clear anodized aluminum curtainwall. • Milk paint • Low-VOC to no-VOC finishes • Custom perforated stainless steel ceilings • FSC-certified engineered wood flooring • Low-VOC carpeting, linoleum • Custom millwork/furniture with FSC-certified wood veneer and wheatboard substrate

PROJECT DESIGN

When it was still a working farm in the nineteenth century, the Brooks Farm existed as a wholly self-sufficient place that used the surrounding prairie's renewable resources to produce its harvest. Now, as home to the Kresge Foundation, the farm's structures have been preserved and connected to a new twenty-first-century building. This approach embeds the new architecture into an iconic landscape and allows for the use a wide range of new, sustainable strategies. The result is an innovative workplace that combines the best of the new and the old.

The design of the Kresge Foundation headquarters integrates three architectural objectives: the restoration of the landmarked nineteenth-century farmhouse complex, the creation of a great workplace, and the development of a holistic sustainable strategy for the entire complex. The challenge was to create a visually integrated whole from these three disparate objectives. The complex is intended to connect natural and manmade elements, both historic and contemporary, to create a workplace that serves as a model for the staff and for those nonprofit organizations that are eligible for Kresge challenge grants. Conceptually, the restored farmhouse buildings sit high above the landscape, floating on a sea of grasses. In contrast, the new building, with two-thirds of its area below grade, is embedded in the restored prairie and strives to become a part of the landscape.

View of the building set into the retention pond on a base made up of gabions. (BK)

The interiors are intended to be an extension of the restored prairie. Certified wood floors echo the natural grasses that surround the building, bringing the sense of the natural environment into the interior. The modular desk systems echo the geometry of the building—a ribbon of metal that passes above, through, and below the datum that is the surface of the prairie. The interior incorporates a number of sustainable strategies that are integrated into the whole. These include a light harvesting system, energy saving system controls, and raised floor air distribution. The building is qualified for a LEED Gold rating and may qualify for a Platinum rating.

The design evolved through a series of brainstorming sessions with staff, board members, and the design team. This process built a commitment to build a place that is more than just an office. It is a place where every element was designed to acknowledge the larger context, from the overall forms of the building to the furniture systems. The result is a seamless, integrated whole.

TOP: Interior office view of the Kresge Foundation Headquarters. (JM)

BOTTOM LEFT: Interior office view of the Kresge Foundation Headquarters, showing daylighting. (JM)

BOTTOM RIGHT: Custom millwork furniture with FSC-certified wood veneer and wheatboard substrate. (BK)

OPPOSITE PAGE: Nighttime view of exterior elevation of courtyard. (BK)

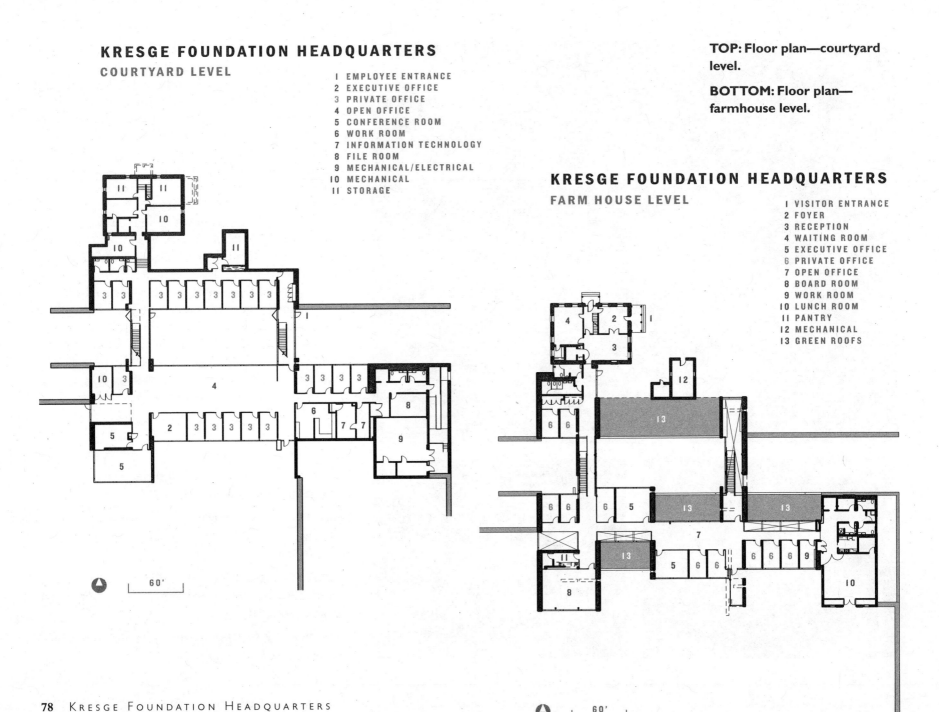

KRESGE FOUNDATION HEADQUARTERS
COURTYARD LEVEL

1 EMPLOYEE ENTRANCE
2 EXECUTIVE OFFICE
3 PRIVATE OFFICE
4 OPEN OFFICE
5 CONFERENCE ROOM
6 WORK ROOM
7 INFORMATION TECHNOLOGY
8 FILE ROOM
9 MECHANICAL/ELECTRICAL
10 MECHANICAL
11 STORAGE

TOP: Floor plan—courtyard level.

BOTTOM: Floor plan—farmhouse level.

KRESGE FOUNDATION HEADQUARTERS
FARM HOUSE LEVEL

1 VISITOR ENTRANCE
2 FOYER
3 RECEPTION
4 WAITING ROOM
5 EXECUTIVE OFFICE
6 PRIVATE OFFICE
7 OPEN OFFICE
8 BOARD ROOM
9 WORK ROOM
10 LUNCH ROOM
11 PANTRY
12 MECHANICAL
13 GREEN ROOFS

60'

60'

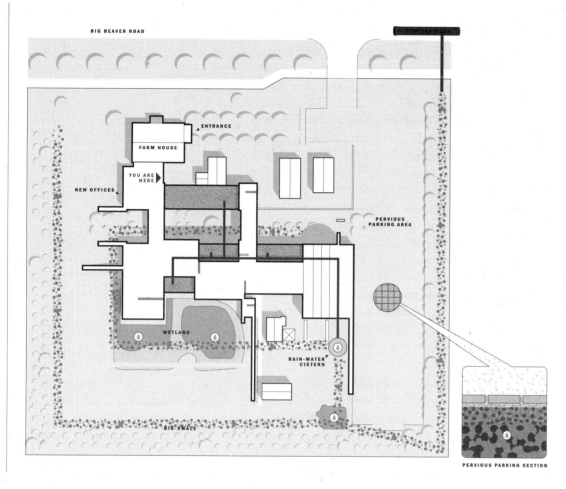

BIG BEAVER ROAD

ENTRANCE

FARM HOUSE

YOU ARE HERE

NEW OFFICES

PERVIOUS PARKING AREA

WETLAND

RAIN-WATER CISTERN

BIO-SWALE

PERVIOUS PARKING SECTION

Water movement.

The Kresge Foundation Headquarters building includes 19,551 square feet of new construction. The existing farm structures, including the farmhouse, barn and sheds, which totaled some 6,562 square feet, were extensively restored and integrated into the overall complex.

PROJECT CONSTRUCTION

During construction, several interesting challenges had to be met. In large part, these were due to the fact that a great deal was happening on a relatively small site. Existing structures were dismantled and their contents recycled, extensive site work was required to create a wetland area, and a geothermal well system was installed. In addition, great care was required while working around and, in some cases, relocating existing historic structures.

Among the most interesting construction features of the Kresge Foundation are the gabion walls. These wire basket–enclosed rubble walls play a key role in several of the sustainable strategies for the building. Gabions are an ancient design, originally used as portable fortifications during medieval times. Wicker frames were hauled to battle sites where they were filled with soil and fieldstone to form instant barricades. The gabions at the Kresge Headquarters are made of heavy-duty wire filled with recycled demolition rubble. These were capped with local crushed granite to form retaining walls near and around the building. The strategic placement of these retaining walls allowed the architects to embed the building into the landscape while still permitting perimeter daylighting in the lower level.

The small site made the extensive recycling program for construction waste a particular challenge. While some of the demolition debris was partially recycled on-site in the gabion walls, most of it was removed to a location where it could be sorted for recycling. Construction waste was also recycled using an off-site sorting process.

A central vision for this project was the preservation and enhancement of the existing farmstead structures. These included the original farmhouse, a barn, and several outbuildings. All of these structures were incorporated into the final design. To take full advantage of their specific attributes, however, all of the buildings except for the farmhouse were moved. Care was taken to move the buildings as little as possible in order to preserve the original sense of the farmstead. Once they were relocated, each of the five structures houses a new use. The barn became an employee lunchroom, the smokehouse houses a mechanical room, one of the sheds houses an emergency generator, and the three remaining sheds are used for storage.

Creative design and careful coordination allowed the design and construction team to overcome significant challenges to meet the client's objectives.

USE

While the Kresge Foundation Headquarters' primary function is as a workplace, it also serves as a compelling demonstration of green design principles for potential grant applicants. As a workplace, the build-ing provides a comfortable environment for foundation staff and visitors, one that supports their unique work activities. At the same time, its systems operate very efficiently. As a demonstration project, it showcases 38 different sustainable strategies. These range from a sophisticated geothermal well heat exchange system to simple bicycle storage and shower areas.

Among the features that make the building a great workplace are the extensive use of controlled daylighting, access to the restored prairie landscape, and wetland development. Staff and visitors enjoy a strong sense of connection with the outdoors that comes, in part, from the building's transparency and its orientation to maximize daylighting without excessive heat gain. The building's two levels, one above and one below grade, are arranged around an open courtyard. The relatively slender profile of the building's two main wings allows both daylight and views to penetrate into both the open and the private offices.

That strong visual connection is enhanced by the proximity of the restored prairie landscape and wetlands and the wide variety of wildlife they attract to the site.

The building's numerous sustainable features posed some initial challenges for its occupants, but the staff quickly learned that the first year of operation would be a commissioning phase as they learned to operate the building properly and as systems were debugged. While there were occasional setbacks, that period endowed the users with a deeper feeling of participation in the movement toward environmental responsibility. This sense of shared mission has been good for the organization.

View of the building set into the retention pond on a base made up of gabions.

Custom millwork furniture with FSC-certified wood veneer and wheatboard substrate.

Detail of window and exposed frame.

A living machine—the Gwinnett Environmental and Heritage Center achieves 75 percent water savings, compared to a building equal in size.

Integrated Corten steel art panels interpreting prairie, wetlands, and woodlands.

Pivoting gallery wall panels allow for the building's long life and loose fit.

CARL T. CURTIS MIDWEST REGIONAL HEADQUARTERS BUILDING NATIONAL PARK SERVICE, U.S. DEPARTMENT OF THE INTERIOR
OMAHA, NEBRASKA

111

The knowledge of sustainable practices by **National Park Service** employees guarantee the maintenance of this structure.

Efficient mechanical system, effected by light-harvesting, low-emissivity glazing, light sensors, and shading, optimize the building's energy performance.

12 WORLD BIRDING CENTER
MISSION, TEXAS

Essential to the design was creating comfortable exterior spaces that connected visitors with the wildlife habitats within the complex.

Ubiquitous to farm buildings throughout the countryside, corrugated metal respects the agricultural context of the region. The use of arched panels for the self-supporting roof allowed for a 48 percent reduction in steel by weight for the project.

The central staircase of unfinished steel provides access to all floors and the rooftop garden.

The square entry courtyard is an informal gathering place and is also used for orientation meetings with new students. The garden is made of river rock excavated from the site and unfinished steel planters filled with indigenous plants.

GEOTHERMAL WELL SYSTEM

The most ambitious sustainable strategy employed in the Kresge Foundation Headquarters building is its geothermal well system. This system of 40 closed-loop wells, each 400 feet deep, is laid out on a 20-foot by 20-foot grid hidden beneath the parking lot. These wells allow the stable ground temperature to help heat the building in winter and cool the building in summer. Water moves through this closed-loop system of 1¼-inch-diameter plastic pipe to three large heat pumps. The heat pumps operate on the same principal as a refrigerator: there are three components to the system—a line filled with a coolant (in this case, water), a compressor, and an expansion valve. The coolant is cool between the expansion valve and the compressor—it picks up heat from the surrounding environment while the coolant is hot between the compressor and the expansion valve, giving off heat to the surrounding environment. The system can move heat to either side of the system.

With a refrigerator, the surrounding environment is the air in the kitchen and the flow of heat is always one way—from inside the refrigerator to the surrounding kitchen. A heat pump, on the other hand, is designed to be able to move heat in both directions; in other words, it could cool the air in the refrigerator or it could heat the air in the refrigerator. In this way the heat pump can heat or cool the building. There are two types of heat pumps—air source and water source. The Kresge Foundation's system is a water source system. The water comes from the geothermal wells. During the summer the heat pumps move heat from the building into the earth, while in the winter heat is moved from the earth into the building. The efficiency of the heat pumps is significantly increased by the use of water at a relatively constant temperature.

During the cooling season the operation of the system slowly raises the temperature in the surrounding soil, while during the heating season the reverse occurs. This fact drives two important aspects of the design. First, the wells must be spaced at least twenty feet apart to avoid heat pollution between wells. Second, the heat extracted must balance the heat rejected during the year. If this does not occur, the temperature of the soil can either increase or decrease over a long period of time with the potential of seriously reducing the efficiency of the system. In fact, one of the key challenges faced by the design team was the relatively poor thermal conductivity of the soils which requires one-third more wells than would have been necessary on a site with better soils.

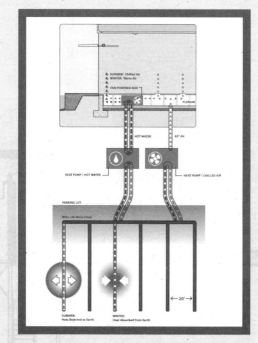

Geothermal diagram.

The geothermal wells are part of a larger strategy to reduce energy consumption. Other elements of this strategy include the building's siting, the thermal performance of the envelope, the daylighting controls, and underfloor air distribution system. The building's siting helps to reduce the need for energy because much of the building is set below grade, which mitigates the seasonal temperature variations. Similarly, the use of green roofs helps to insulate the building from solar gain during the summer. The orientation of the building, which allows for control of the daylight that enters the building, is seasonally responsive, permitting more solar gain in the winter when it helps heat the space and less in the summer, when that heat is not wanted.

A high-performance building enclosure also helps to reduce the load on heating and air conditioning systems. The underfloor ducting distributes conditioned air efficiently and allows for individual control.

Taken together, these combined strategies are what made the geothermal system practical and feasible.

GWINNETT ENVIRONMENTAL & HERITAGE CENTER
BUFORD, GEORGIA

Completed:	September 2006
Owner:	Gwinnett County
Architects:	Lord, Aeck & Sargent
Consultants:	Lose & Associates, Inc.—Civil
	Uzun & Case Engineers—Structural
	Newcomb & Boyd—MEP
	The Jaeger Company—Landscape Architecture
	Van Sickle & Rolleri—Exhibit Design
	Rocky Mountain Institute—Daylighting and Energy Consultant
General Contractor:	Juneau Construction Company
Photographer:	Jonathan Hillyer
Site:	The project is located on over 200 acres of preserved, forested park land—a previously undeveloped greenfield site.
Environment:	Suburban
Program:	The two-story, 59,000 gross-square-foot Gwinnett Environmental & Heritage Center (GEHC) blends indoor and outdoor classroom space, exterior trails and exhibits, a collection of permanent and rotating displays, and interactive learning opportunities.
Square Footage:	59,000 square feet

Groundwater recharge and infiltration—six drought-resistant blossoming sedums control water absorption on the 40,000-square-foot vegetated roof. Varieties that thrive in a more arid climate were planted at the roof's pitch; varieties that favored wet soil were planted at the bottom of the pitch, where water tends to collect and puddle.

Sustainable Features:

- Use of nonpotable reuse water for irrigation, toilets, and cooling shoals water feature
- Waterless urinals and high-efficiency faucets achieving a 76 percent reduction in potable water use
- Natural stormwater management features including an acre of green roof, four different types of porous paving, bioswales, and rain gardens
- Extensive use of daylighting with automated daylight harvesting controls (achieving a 2 percent daylight factor in 81 percent of occupied spaces)
- High-efficiency lighting with daylight sensors (combination of T5, T8, and metal halide lighting, yielding a lighting power density of 1.04 W/ft^2)
- Passive heating/cooling utilizing deep overhangs, external shading devices, operable exhaust louvers, and a vegetated roof to reduce solar gain
- Improved thermal envelope with increased wall insulation and high-efficiency glazing (0.3 U-value)
- High-efficiency mechanical system with innovative cooling shoals water feature that reduces cooling tower load

Waterways of interactive learning—visitors and employees can access the water feature that runs under the building and is used for partially cooling the center.

View looking into the teaching lab, dining room, and lecture hall.

Structural System:

- Modular structural bay of load-bearing, parallel walls with clerestory windows above
- Load-bearing exterior walls of cast-in-place concrete clad in recycled granite
- Extensive sloping green roof on Tectum deck and factory-fabricated wood trusses

Mechanical System:

- High-efficiency mechanical equipment was used including 16.72 EER chillers
- Innovative cooling shoals site water feature that reduces the cooling tower load by circulating the water feature through plate heat exchangers in the mechanical system

Materials:

- Recycled granite waste from monument production
- Porous paving with aggregate recharge beds
- Native Southern yellow pine exposed roof framing
- Native regional plant species on-site with drought-resistant sedums on the green roof
- Low-emitting paints, adhesives, sealants, and carpet systems
- Copper rainchains

PROJECT DESIGN

Over the past 10 years, Gwinnett County—part of the Atlanta metropolitan area—has been one of the fastest-growing counties in the country. Recognizing that this growth would place tremendous strain on water resources, county officials planned and built a state-of-the-art wastewater treatment plant on a 700-acre tract of land. As a further commitment to management of the vital water resource, county officials created the Gwinnett Environmental & Heritage Center (GEHC) on the wooded site to improve education on the critical role that water plays in daily life.

The GEHC, which was developed through a collaboration of the Gwinnett County Board of Commissioners, the Gwinnett County Public School System, and the University of Georgia (UGA) College of Environment & Design, teaches about the importance of water. The center's programs and interactive exhibits—designed for K-12 and adult audiences—explore the impact that water has had on our history and everyday lives as well as the water management challenges we will face in the future.

The team began the project with a goal of achieving the LEED Silver level of certification, with a specific energy optimization goal of 30 percent better than ASHRAE 90.1-1999. Iterative energy modeling, using DOE-2.2 (eQUEST v3.44), was conducted during the schematic design and design development stages in order to optimize the project's design and achieve the energy performance target. The design exceeded the target, achieving a 39 percent reduction in energy use and LEED Gold certification. The project was sited and massed to minimize im-

ABOVE: Detail of window and exposed roof frame.

OPPOSITE: High-efficiency lamps help the building meet 1.04 watts per square foot of power density where artificial light is needed.

pact to the natural surroundings. At the beginning of the design process, the 233-acre site was investigated by the owner, architect, and landscape architect to identify a project site that would minimize the need for grading while maintaining most of the existing tree canopy for shading. Site plans were developed with the intent to minimize the area of disturbance and to maximize permeable areas within the development zone. While the vast majority of the site is hardwood and mixed pine/hardwood forest, the area chosen for parking was an area of more recent pine growth. The parking was located on a relatively flat area of the generally hilly property, with the building spanning an adjacent ravine. The ravine became a cascading water feature that draws nonpotable reuse water from the nearby wastewater treatment facility and uses it to provide air-conditioning. Throughout the schematic design and design development phases, charrettes were conducted with the full design team, owner team, and various user groups and stakeholders. While it's not uncommon to gather the owner and user stakeholders for museum/interpretive projects, it was unusual to involve the entire design team and to demonstrate sustainability as a core element of the project.

The building's unique cooling shoals water feature that helps to air-condition the building came directly out of these integrated design charrettes. The landscape architect brought up the idea of a water feature given the project's focus on water, the owner brought up the potential to use nonpotable reuse water from the plant, and the architect and mechanical engineer came up with the idea of using the feature to air-condition the building. These wonderful synergies can only happen when everyone is at the table.

PROJECT CONSTRUCTION

As a result of the integrated nature of the design process, with the full consultant team involved from project's inception, there was far more communication and collaboration during the construction phase. All of the team members were involved in developing the vision for the facility. As in any typical construction process, it is the architect's responsibility to explicate the building design to the contractor and assure the owner that the design intent has been faithfully executed. Many of the sustainable design features of the Gwinnett project required special construction phase coordination involving the design team's hands-on involvement. This was one of the general contractor's first LEED-designed buildings and they were excited about the project and willing to be flexible with design input throughout the construction phase. The construction agreement was "design-bid-build," so continuous correspondence was necessary so that the special detailing could be properly executed without incurring unexpected, additional costs. The team's commitment to work together to realize the project's intended design was necessary to make this project so successful both in terms of sustainability and aesthetics.

The roof system itself was a challenge for both the construction and design teams. To help ensure that the soil was properly stabilized on the slope, the plantings for the 40,000-square-foot roof were grown ahead of their planned installation and the entire system, including the landscaping, flashings, roofing membrane, and insulation, were completely covered by the specified single source warranty. The final product is true to the design document's intent but details related to the soil stabilization and plant

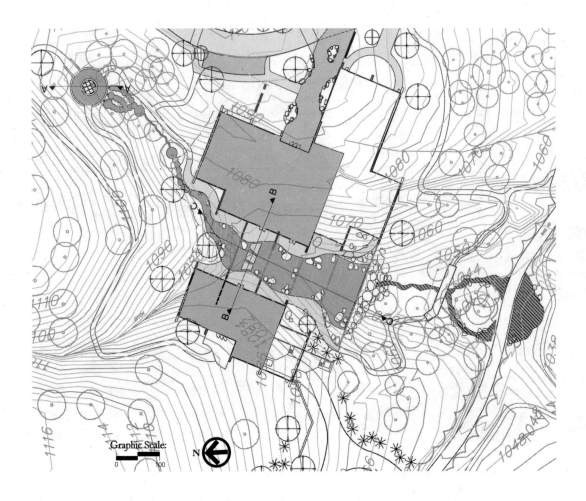

Site plan.

species reflect a collaborative effort by the manufacturer's installers, design team, and owner.

Another challenge that required extra efforts by both the design team and the contractor relates to the mechanical system. The design called for all ductwork serving the upper public areas to be from the lower level so that the open structure and windows were free of any HVAC equipment. This meant that

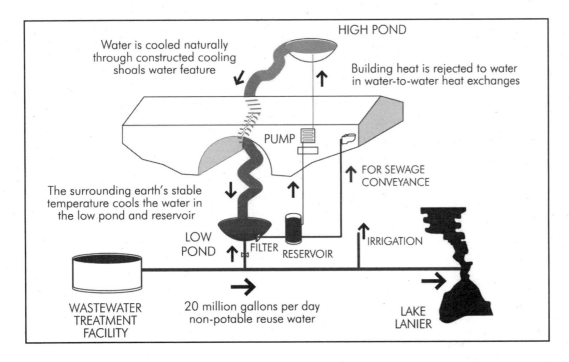

HIGH POND

Water is cooled naturally
through constructed cooling
shoals water feature

Building heat is rejected to water
in water-to-water heat exchanges

PUMP

The surrounding earth's stable
temperature cools the water in
the low pond and reservoir

FOR SEWAGE
CONVEYANCE

LOW
POND

FILTER

RESERVOIR

IRRIGATION

WASTEWATER
TREATMENT
FACILITY

20 million gallons per day
non-potable reuse water

LAKE
LANIER

Cooling shoals water feature diagram. The facility's signature integrated design feature, a unique reuse water feature, sprang directly from the charrettes. The landscape architect proposed a water feature, the owner suggested using nonpotable reuse water from the adjacent plant, and the architect envisioned using the feature to condition the building.

all of the ductwork had to be routed along the east-west column lines where long, narrow chases were formed through the concrete floor structure or in a subconcrete floor duct system; both options are unusual to typical construction projects.

PROJECT USE

The mission of the Gwinnett Environmental & Heritage Center is to serve as a recreational catalyst for inspiring and engaging community involvement in educating Gwinnett's students to solve tomorrow's environmental challenges; to promote sustainable development practices and the utilization of new technologies; and to enhance the appreciation of Gwinnett's natural resources.

Given the mission, the county had criteria to incorporate into the scope of work to address sustainability as a way of life. As such, various aspects of the building were required to address energy conservation, sustainable building resource products, and water conservation. In addition, the county wanted a building dedicated to hands-on learning as a real-world example of what the average citizen could implement. As the GEHC executive director said, "We wanted features that would illustrate to the development community that you can have a beautiful building with ecologically sound options that—although they may cost more initially—will save money in the long term."

The building has met all of the demands of the client and provides the citizens of Gwinnett and the Southeastern region with a facility that expands on the mission of the center. It has enhanced the staff's ability to provide a broad range of environmental education programs. At the same time, by committing to the LEED certification process as a catalyst to create applications of sustainable design ideas, the client and the design team created a project that met the challenges and maximized the opportunities of its site.

From the moment a visitor enters the building until the minute they walk out the doors, they are immersed in the workings of a compelling example of sustainability. Students, elected officials, and citizens have all been mesmerized by the innovation and foresight of the design team. As a consequence, both the client and the public have a greater awareness of how user-friendly and efficient sustainable architecture can be.

WATER MANAGEMENT

A teaching laboratory—promoting sustainability as a way of thought and practice, students and visitors learn the critical role water plays in daily life, history, and the challenges that face our future.

Gwinnett County is one of the fastest-growing counties in the country. Recognizing that this growth would place tremendous strain on water resources, county officials created the Gwinnett Environmental & Heritage Center (GEHC) to improve education about the critical role that water plays in daily life. The GEHC's programs and interactive exhibits explore the impact that water has had on our history and everyday lives, as well as the water management challenges we will face in the future. "This will be a place where visitors can learn about the essential role water plays in our lives, where they can learn a little bit more about our community's history, and where people can just enjoy nature," says F. Wayne Hill, former chairman of the Gwinnett County Commission.

The building embodies the principles of water conservation and education not just through its programs but through its very design. It is projected to use 76 percent less potable water and 39 percent less energy than a conventional building.

The project's environmental goals and strategies were developed specifically to respond to regional environmental challenges. Three major challenges are limited potable water supply (the Atlanta Regional Commission predicts that water will be the resource that limits the region's growth), polluted stormwater (due to the erosion and increased runoff associated with rapid development), and poor urban air quality (due to the urban heat island effect and air pollution from the region's coal-fired power plants).

A green roof was anticipated from the project's earliest inception given its dual benefits of reducing the urban heat island effect, as well as naturally reducing and treating stormwater runoff. Porous paving and natural stormwater management features were used throughout the site, resulting in no increase in the postdevelopment runoff rate when compared to the predevelopment greenfield site.

Several features were incorporated to increase groundwater recharge and infiltration. The green roof is the most visible feature. Planted with six species of flowering, drought-resistant sedums, the plantings help directly combat the urban heat island effect, and actually use and absorb water that otherwise would have contributed to stormwater runoff. Because of the roof's steep pitch, varieties suited to more arid soil were planted at the height of the pitch and varieties able to thrive in wet soil were planted toward the bottom of the pitch, where water may collect and puddle. These plants are very hardy and require low maintenance and little irrigation after their establishment into the growth material. An isolated 800-square-foot area of the green roof is dedicated to granite outcrop plants native to this region of Georgia.

Another feature attributing to a reduction in stormwater runoff includes the porous paving used on-site. Four different types of porous paving with aggregate recharge beds are used to reduce runoff. These surfaces absorb excess rainwater into the ground, allowing it to percolate naturally back into the aquifer instead of being collected while hot and polluted by storm sewer structures and sent out of the region via overburdened streams. Any excess runoff from the green roof and porous paving is directed into bioswales and two detention areas planted with native wetland species. Rain chains are used at the eaves of the building to slow and direct the water into the bioswales rather than the traditional downspouts. The rain chains provide an element of beauty and become an interpretive element inside and out. There is no net increase in stormwater rate from the predeveloped conditions. All site plantings are regionally native and are located based on typical plant communities and onsite microclimates.

Nonpotable water from the adjacent treatment plant is used for irrigation, via a drip irrigation system. The bathrooms have waterless urinals and low-flow (0.5 gpm), automatic lavatory faucets, and the toilets are flushed with clean, nonpotable reuse waste water effluent from the nearby treatment facility (for the first such installation in the state, see the Water Feature Diagram). The calculated water efficiency accounts for a 76 percent reduction as compared with a standard system. Together, these sewage conveyance and water sav-

A living machine—the Gwinnett Environmental and Heritage Center achieves 75 percent water savings, compared to a building equal in size.

ing strategies are projected to save 316,000 gallons of potable water annually.

This building, by design and in response to the sustainable considerations, is a living machine. One of the most challenging aspects of the design was fine-tuning the recirculating exterior reuse water feature. This feature provides the primary cooling for the building's chilled water loop; its functionality and control, which would normally be a landscape system, were carefully integrated into the energy management system controls.

MARION ARTS AND ENVIRONMENTAL CENTER AT LOWE PARK

10

MARION, IOWA

Completed:	May 2006
Owner:	City of Marion—Marion, Iowa
Architects:	RDG Planning & Design
Consultants:	Anderson Bogert—Civil Engineers
	Charles Saul—Structural Engineers
	RDG Planning & Design—MEP Engineering
	RDG Planning & Design—Lighting Design
General Contractor:	Miron Construction
Photographer:	Kun Zhang
Site:	Development of the first phase of a 180-acre park which includes the restoration of the first 40 acres to native Iowa prairie and the development of an art and environment center and associated play space and community gardens.
Environment:	Rural, agricultural land

Entrance hall glows on the landscape like a farm structure. All site lighting is controlled with a time clock and multilevel lamping.

Program:	The art and environment building is intended as a simple farm structure within the suburban edge of a small community in east central Iowa. The simple timber structure is designed to allow the building to glow from within when approached at night and to allow for views from the interior to the Iowa prairie landscape during the day. The building is designed to demonstrate sustainable strategies and is designed to LEED-certified standards. The project therefore considers the land as inextricably linked to the systems of the building much like the original farms of Iowa.
Square Footage:	11,500 square feet
Sustainable Features:	• Geothermal heat pump system • Sewage treated with a wetlands septic system • The play space utilizing only site stormwater for the small pond structure • Rainwater collected in rain barrels for use on-site • Site restored to Iowa tall grass prairie • Stormwater managed through bioswales • Local limestone utilized for building facades and interiors • Supplemental heat from a corn-burning fireplace insert • Ground and polished colored concrete floors
Structural System:	• Glue-laminated timber roof construction • SIP panels that are created from waste products from wheat production
Mechanical System:	• Heating and cooling of the facility is from a geothermal heat pump system yielding energy savings of approximately 40 percent
Materials:	• Corten steel • Cedar siding • Locally quarried stone • Wood windows • Ground and polished concrete with fly ash additive • Formaldehyde-free cabinetry

PROJECT DESIGN

The City of Marion, part of the Cedar Rapids metro area in east central Iowa, was given 180 acres of farmland by a local businessman, George Lowe. While the parcel had originally been slated for a single-family subdivision, Mr. Lowe ultimately decided that donating the property to the city for the purpose of creating a park dedicated to art and environmental education and conservation would serve a greater purpose. The larger plan for the property also includes areas for community festivals, an intermediate school for the community (not part of this project), and recreation fields.

The Marion Arts and Environmental Center is part of the first phase of development of the land, which also includes an associated play space, community gardens, and the restoration of 40 acres to native Iowa prairie. The building itself includes a gathering space with corn-burning stove, a small gallery and art studio, Marion Parks and Recreation offices, multipurpose rooms for community use, and a small dining area for daily meals for local senior residents.

The design of the building recalls a farm building set within the restored prairie. The building is sited on an east–west axis to promote natural ventilation and to maximize the connection to the sun to the south and north daylight. The east and west exposures are minimized to reduce heat gain—particularly from the west. Natural ventilation is promoted in a number of ways. First, the shallow floor plan promotes cross

Exposed Agriboard®—structural insulated panels (SIPs) used for roof structure. Wheat bales used for internal insulation between OSB layers.

ventilation. Second, the number of *core* or internal rooms that cannot benefit from natural ventilation has been minimized and programmed to be lightly occupied. Finally, the building is designed to bring in air down low on the south and exit high on the north. The basic shape of the building has been tailored to allow for natural ventilation from the southern prevailing breezes in the spring–fall months.

The building's east–west orientation also maximizes northern daylight and southern daylight into the facility through operable windows. Daylighting is a major strategy for energy conservation in the building and in many ways defines the shape of the building. These windows are located as high as possible within spaces for deep daylight penetration. To control the sun exposure, these windows are shaded with overhangs and Cor-Ten steel fins to reduce heat gain through the glass surfaces. More glass than typical is used in the central gathering space to allow for a meaningful connection to the natural prairie, the natural play space to the east, and to the rolling Iowa landscape in the distance. All occupied spaces within the building have access to natural daylight and exterior views.

PROJECT CONSTRUCTION

In order to achieve the sustainable goals set out for the project, a holistic approach was adopted in the construction of the building that combines a number of design strategies and material selections. The roof structure is made from exposed engineered lumber (large wood beams that are built up from smaller pieces). The roof deck is made of structural insulated

ABOVE: Gypsum board used for interior surfaces with high recycled content. Corn-burning stove insert in fireplace to supplement foyer heating in winter.

TOP LEFT: Vernacular entry with native vegetation, viewing and daylighting windows, and cedar siding with panelized cedar shakes.

BOTTOM LEFT: Integrated Corten steel art panels interpreting prairie, wetlands, and woodlands.

ABOVE: Pivoting gallery wall panels allow for the building's long life and loose fit.

TOP RIGHT: The building engages the discovery garden with native Anamosa limestone quarried 30 miles from site.

BOTTOM RIGHT: North facade illustrating daylighting windows and viewing windows in evening.

panels (or SIPs) that are created from waste products from wheat production in Texas. Oriented strand-board (OSB) is used as the stressed skins with wheat straw to make the insulation contained within the SIP panel. This is also a renewable resource for insulation. The timbers are stained with a low-VOC natural-soy stain and the SIP panels are left exposed, with no finish. Painting is kept to a minimum in the facility. The stone used in the building is from a local quarry within 30 miles and is not highly cut or polished. Minimal effort was used to cut the stone for use in the building. A very small portion of the project utilizes carpet. Carpet is used only in the offices, which represents approximately 10 percent of the building's usable space. All other occupied spaces utilize ground and polished concrete that has fly ash as an additive as a cement reducer in the mix. All cabinetry in the building is fabricated without formaldehyde-based glues.

The building is projected to conserve 40 to 50 percent of the energy of a code-compliant building of the same type designed to code in Iowa. This is achieved using a number of strategies. First, the envelope is designed with higher insulation values and energy efficient windows. The envelope is also designed to be tight and enabled to dry to the exterior for the Iowa climate. Second, as discussed before, the shape of the building and the use of windows in every occupied space allows for daylighting, which reduces the need for electric lighting. The lighting that is provided is energy efficient and controlled by occupancy and photocell sensors. Third, the building utilizes a geothermal heat pump system that uses the earth's soil temperature as a heat sink for heating and cooling the facility. The loads for the building using this all-electric system are more consistent year-round and

reduce the impact on peak cooling loads in the summer. In addition, natural gas or oil is not used for heating on-site. The building is all-electric and the energy provider is currently investing in renewable wind energy in Iowa. While there are no current contracts in place for purchasing green power for the building to date, they will be accommodated in the future. The heat pump system is zoned to allow for a dynamic system that can accommodate fluctuating use of space throughout a day or week. Fourth, for supplemental heating in winter, the main gathering space can be heated with a corn-burning stove/furnace. In the coldest of Iowa weeks, the furnace would use approximately one bushel of shelled corn per day. This corn is obviously a renewable resource and is demonstrating to the public that there are options to traditional fossil fuel heating and cooling systems.

PROJECT USE

The intentions for the use of Lowe Park are centered in the demonstrational aspects of the project for the local community and Iowa in general. The project is intended to show that modest, practical decisions that consider the humble, local aspects of sustainability have as much promise as expensive, highly technological and expensive solutions.

As a result, the center's educational mission focuses on communicating to visitors the importance as well as the accessibility of sustainable buildings.

Discovery garden utilizes site stormwater and fluctuates seasonally.

The center's educational mission also shows that there are many techniques that can be applied to people's daily lives.

The sustainable design of this project begins with the conservation of the native Iowa prairie—active farms remain to the north of this project and its restored prairie/park. Conceptually, the building is another farm structure within the neighborhood inextricably linked to its surroundings. The land provides the heating and cooling of the facility through a geothermal heat pump system. It provides the waste wheat for the roof insulation which is created from waste products contained within structural insulated panels. It also provides both for natural sewage processing through a wetlands septic system, and on-site stormwater runoff management. The site uses all rainfall on-site. When it rains, roof water is collected in rain barrels and used for irrigation, leaving no need for a lawn sprinkler system. All of the landscaping involves native species that require no additional water beyond typical rainfall. Also, the majority of the site is restored to prairie that absorbs water and eliminates runoff. Rainwater assists in the wetlands septic system processing. All of the water around the eastern one-half of the building is drained to the water feature in the children's play space to the east of the facility. The City of Marion has committed to the notion that in dry seasons, when it becomes a dry river bed, it will not be filled with potable water. During rainy seasons, the water feature becomes a natural amenity in the garden. It helps demonstrate water and water usage to those visiting the site. Also, toilets are kept to a minimum with portable systems being used for large events. The toilet facilities within the building are low consumption and are only provided for typical building occupants.

The energy and associated cost analysis indicated an estimated payback of energy-related design items at three to five years beyond code-based systems. This included the incremental additional costs for the ground-source heat pump system, additional insulation values, daylighting systems and controls, increased window to wall area for daylighting, and energy efficient windows.

The project is designed to serve the Marion community for at least 100 years if the building is maintained properly. The building is designed to be fairly easily deconstructed at the end of its life through the use of exposed timber and SIP panels without a lot of ancillary ceilings. Exposed concrete floors can be pulverized at the end of the building's life to be used for future concrete on other projects. The building was designed with large, open rooms that have no highly specific purpose. The rooms should be used for multiple functions over the life of the facility. The project achieves the appropriate balance between budget, need, and resultant size of spaces. Each space is designed for the average anticipated group in the community and not the largest group that may use spaces infrequently. The materials were selected for their long-term durability.

The building is intended to sit humbly within the prairie and utilize simple and practical sustainable design strategies that speak directly to the local environment.

TOP: Site plan showing general sustainable site, stormwater, black water, and geothermal well fields.

BOTTOM: Floor plan—organized into zones with heat pump system for maximum efficiency.

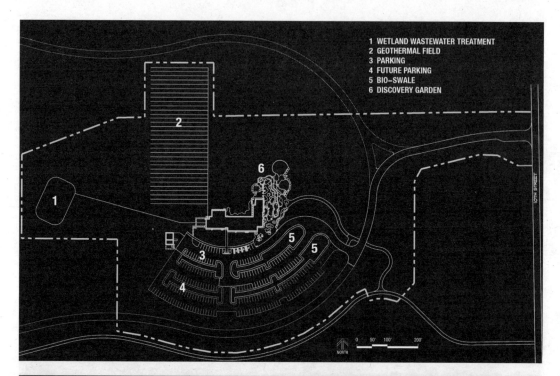

1 WETLAND WASTEWATER TREATMENT
2 GEOTHERMAL FIELD
3 PARKING
4 FUTURE PARKING
5 BIO-SWALE
6 DISCOVERY GARDEN

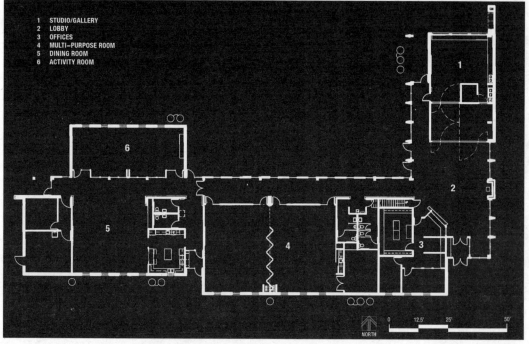

1 STUDIO/GALLERY
2 LOBBY
3 OFFICES
4 MULTI-PURPOSE ROOM
5 DINING ROOM
6 ACTIVITY ROOM

The Marion Arts and Environmental Center at Lowe Park was conceived as a humble structure within a restored Iowa prairie and built on a modest budget. Designed in 2003 and completed in 2006, this 11,865-square-foot facility and the associated park was constructed for $2.8 million dollars, with future expansion planned. LEED certification for the building is also anticipated.

The structure is made of local and regional materials constructed with techniques typical of Midwestern rural farm structures. The building is placed within the restored tall-grass prairie and provides a setting for connecting art and nature through community festivals, visiting artist courses, and environmental discovery play spaces. This midwestern ethic of sustainability through modest materials and methods informed many of the decisions made during the design and construction process. One critical component in the sustain approach to the center's design was right-sizing both the building and the required systems. This strategy generated a number of cost reductions as compared with a conventional building. Following are a number of examples of this strategy.

Daylighting is a major strategy for energy conservation in the building and in many ways defines the shape of the building. Windows are located as high as possible within spaces for deep daylight penetration. To control sun, these windows are shaded with overhangs and corten steel fins to reduce heat gain through the glass surfaces. This allows for the implementation of minimal lighting.

The primary heating and cooling of the facility is from a geothermal heat pump system yielding energy savings of approximately 40 to 50 percent. In order to reduce the required size for the system, supplemental heat comes from a corn-burning fireplace insert. With regard to plumbing, toilets are kept to a code minimum with portable systems being used for large events.

Prior to the construction of the Arts and Environmental Center, the site was a corn and soybean field that had been master planned for typical suburban residential development. In lieu of this proposed

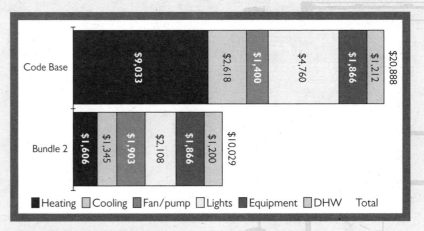

Building Energy Performance.

development, the owner donated the property to the City of Marion Parks Foundation for use as a public park dedicated to art and environmental learning. As such, the site design decisions were guided by notions of demonstrating simple and more affordable sustainable site design techniques to the public.

First, the site grading work was kept to a minimum and included only the area required for immediate construction of the necessary drives, parking, and building construction. Second, rainfall on the site is collected and reused both as part of a wetlands septic system and as a water feature in the children's play space. During rainy seasons, the water feature becomes a natural amenity in the garden. It helps demonstrate water and water usage to those visiting the site.

The landscaping features only native species that require no additional water beyond typical rainfall; no permanent irrigation system is needed. Also, the majority of the site has been restored to prairie. This absorbs water and eliminates runoff—a significant problem in Iowa and on this site prior to this project.

All of these design decisions have significantly reduced the costs associated with managing and maintaining the park environment.

CARL T. CURTIS MIDWEST REGIONAL HEADQUARTERS BUILDING NATIONAL PARK SERVICE, U.S. DEPARTMENT OF THE INTERIOR

OMAHA, NEBRASKA

Completed:	July 2004
Owner:	Park Service Developers/Noddle Development Company
Architects:	LEO A DALY
Consultants:	Kirkham Michael Consulting Engineers—Civil Engineers
	LEO A DALY—Structural Engineers
	LEO A DALY—MEP Engineers
	LEO A DALY— Interior Designers
	Purdy & Slack Architects, P.C.—Landscape Architects
	HNTB Architecture—LEED Advisor
	LEO A DALY—LEED Documentation
	M.E. Group, Inc.—Commissioning Agent
General Contractor:	Kiewit Construction Company
Photographer:	Tom Kessler, Kessler Photography
Site:	The building is located on the bank of the Missouri River in Omaha, Nebraska.
Environment:	Urban

The Carl T. Curtis Midwest Regional Headquarters houses the offices from which the National Park Service oversees a 13-state region. It is Nebraska's first LEED Gold-certified building.

Program:

The facility, which provides a new home for the Midwest Regional Office of the National Park Service, needed to meet the following design goals. First, it had to provide the resources to support the 13 states it serves. Second, it needed to act as a sustainable design teaching tool of the National Park Service. Third, it had to relate the history of the river and the region and their importance to the area and its future. Finally, it needed to complement the riverfront redevelopment while helping to define its identity.

Square Footage:

67,000 square feet

Sustainable Features:

- Windows use high U-value glass that allows daylight in but greatly reduces the amount of incoming heat and harmful UV rays.
- Extensive utilization of natural lighting
- Levels two and three of the building have horizontal sunscreens on the south and east sides to further increase thermal efficiency.
- The building sits on an east–west axis—this provides access to exterior views for more than 90 percent of the interior workspaces.
- The project uses light-harvesting technology with sensors that measure the natural light in occupied spaces and adjust the electrical lighting accordingly.
- The parking lot surface and walkways surrounding the building use a light-colored concrete that reduces the heat island effect.
- More than 75 percent of the roof surface features a special white thermoplastic roofing material that reduces building heat gain.
- Native plants—such as buffalo grass, black-eyed Susans, and cottonwood trees—surround the building, and within two years after planting, the landscaping does require watering.
- The use of low-flow shower heads, waterless urinals, dual-flush toilets, low-flow lavatories, and lavatories with autosensors reduces water consumption.
- More than 60 percent of construction waste from demolition, construction, and land clearing was diverted by means of recycling.
- More than 10 percent of the total project materials and products were made from recycled content materials.
- More than 20 percent of the materials for the project, including Kansas limestone, came from within 500 miles of the project site, and more than half were sourced or extracted locally.

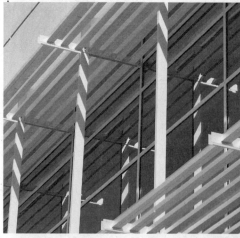

- Almost all of the wood used was acquired from forests approved by the Forest Stewardship Council.
- The building interior uses raised flooring with underfloor air distribution.
- Automatic digital control system monitors and allows for adjustment of all building systems, including air temperature and humidity.
- The parking lot contains several 110-volt AC power outlets that may be used by commuters to recharge electric-powered vehicles. The parking also area features priority spaces set aside for carpoolers.
- Secure bicycle storage and shower and locker facilities on-site.

Structural System:
- The building utilizes a posttensioned concrete framework consisting of columns, girders, beams, and deck.

Mechanical System:
- The facility uses a rooftop air-cooled chiller serving a VAV air-handling unit.
- Air is delivered below the floor by underfloor VAV boxes.
- A central exhaust, carbon dioxide detection, and building automation systems also are incorporated into the design.

Materials:
- Insulated precast concrete wall panels
- Steel siding
- Low-E insulated tinted glass
- Kansas cottonwood limestone accent wall
- White thermoplastic membrane roofing and standing seam metal roofing
- Stained concrete flooring
- Cast-in-place concrete columns, beams, and underside of floor slabs
- Maple casework and doors, with natural finish
- Exposed steel beams
- Kansas Tuxedo Gray limestone countertops

TOP: Many of the materials were left in a "raw" state.

CENTER: Glass curtain walls consist of fully recyclable glass and aluminum; the wall covering is made from recycled plastic soda bottles.

BOTTOM: The design team created an on-site ecosystem consisting entirely of plant life native to the eastern Nebraska prairie landscape—buffalo grass, black-eyed Susans, and cottonwood trees—that lend to self-sustained vegetation, requiring no irrigation.

PROJECT DESIGN

The Carl T. Curtis Midwest Regional Headquarters for the National Park Service stands on the banks of the Missouri River in downtown Omaha. With its philosophies about the environment in mind, the National Park Service engaged a multidisciplinary design team to create a building that would incorporate a wide array of sustainable features and act as a showcase for green architecture. The performance of these features earned the headquarters its title as the first LEED Gold-certified building in Nebraska from the U.S. Green Building Council's Leadership in Energy and Environmental Design program.

The three-story 67,000-square-foot building sits on 4.67 acres along the Missouri riverfront in a redevelopment area that links various waterside projects. The facility combines its advanced sustainable technology with a classic design approach that allows it to blend seamlessly with the neighboring urban landscape.

The building exterior combines a palette of Kansas Cottonwood limestone and smooth precast concrete walls with abundant glazing. The mechanical and electrical rooms have been located in the west block of the building, which allows for a feeling of transparency throughout all levels of the south, east, and north elevations. The first floor is recessed and acts as one large, flowing curve of glass, which recalls the movement of the river. The north facade has individual structural bays with raised roofs that add to the building's vertical proportion while embracing views of the riverfront and the new pedestrian bridge over the Missouri River.

The design and construction of this project was specifically geared to conserve, protect, and restore its local environment. The building's strategic placement on an east-west axis offers views to the river, ponds, teaching gardens, and city trail systems. This provides the building occupants with a constant reminder of the sustainable environment around them. The building's environmentally friendly material palette minimizes the number of materials and finishes used and features a number of unprocessed materials in their natural states as well as recycled and recyclable materials. These choices help to maximize efficiency and reduce consumption of natural resources.

The parking lot surface and walkways surrounding the building use a light-colored concrete that reduces the heat island effect. Shade trees planted throughout the site also help to shield the building from the sun's heat. The roof was finished with a white thermoplastic roofing material that reduces building heat gain and the necessary size of the HVAC system. High U-value glass in the windows, light-harvesting technology, sunshades, and an underfloor air distribution system also help to reduce overall energy use by 25 percent over standard expenditure.

Additionally, the building supports water conservation with a self-sustaining landscape and water efficient fixtures in the restrooms. The use of native, drought-tolerant plants, such as buffalo grass, black-eyed Susans, and cottonwood trees, that will not require irrigation after the first two years following their planting, also aids in water preservation. Furthermore, the design encourages alternative methods of transportation by including power outlets for electric-powered vehicles, bicycle storage areas, showers and changing areas, and reserved carpool parking spaces.

TOP: The knowledge of sustainable practices by National Park Service employees guarantee the maintenance of this structure.

BOTTOM: The raised floor system transmits heating and cooling directly to occupants, resulting in an estimated 16.8 percent peak-cooling-load reduction and 50 percent peak-heating-load reduction compared to the base building scenario.

PROJECT CONSTRUCTION

The design team of LEO A DALY collaborated closely with Park Service Developers/Noddle Development Company, as well as Kiewit Construction Company, to develop the Carl T. Curtis Midwest Regional Headquarters for the U.S. National Park Service. All project team members, including end users, architects, engineers, contractor, owner, and commissioning authority, committed to the General Service Administration's (GSA) goal of achieving Silver-level LEED certification. With the encouragement of the project development company, team members ultimately sought to surpass GSA's requirements to strive for LEED Gold certification.

All aspects of the construction were carefully coordinated to maximize the sustainability of the building. More than 20 percent of the materials utilized for the exterior as well as the interior of the building, including concrete, steel, and Kansas limestone, were obtained from local sources. Additionally, the Forest Stewardship Council certified almost all of the wood used in this project.

The team also eliminated a great amount of project waste with strategic design and construction methods. The insulated precast panels that serve as both the interior and exterior wall reduced material use by providing a finished interior surface that eliminated the need for stud and sheet rock walls. Stained concrete flooring was used in the public spaces instead of tile. The materials selected for this project are durable, reduce the need for maintenance, and encourage longevity.

The recycling program established for this building was heavily emphasized during construction. More than 60 percent of the construction waste from packaging, construction debris, and land clearing was recycled. This saved on dumping costs by reducing the amount of waste sent to the landfill. Additionally, the project designers selected interior materials, including the curtain walls, solid surface countertops, wall coverings, and carpeting, based on their recyclable content.

Structural, mechanical, and electrical systems for the facility were selected both for their environmental performance and for their flexibility. The building uses a posttensioned concrete framework consisting of columns, girders, beams, and decks. Inside, the first floor is structural instead of slab on grade. All three floors feature a raised floor system to facilitate underfloor distribution of the mechanical, electrical, and voice/data systems to the designated locations. Furthermore, the building uses a 480-V voltage power system to reduce line losses and improve distribution efficiency.

The City of Omaha leased the land where the headquarters is located to Noddle Development Company, which has subleased it to GSA and the U.S. National Park Service. Prior to construction, Native Americans performed a blessing ceremony to emphasize that the particular bank of the Missouri River along which the building is located is sacred to Omaha's heritage.

PROJECT USE

The Carl T. Curtis Midwest Regional Headquarters houses the National Park Service offices that oversee the parks and cultural resources of a 13-state region. The building also serves as headquarters for the Lewis and Clark National Historic Trail, and has a year-round visitor center. In addition, the sustainable design qualities of this building aim to educate the public about the National Park Service's philosophies on the natural environment as well as their stewardship of the cultural environment.

Owners, architects, and end users planned the headquarters to be a vital link within the surrounding Missouri riverfront development master plan, which is comprised of restaurants, a marina, a corporate campus, entertainment venues, and a new recreational trail. Another feature of the headquarters is a teaching garden that educates the public about the natural landscape and vegetation of Nebraska as well as its uses for the local Native Americans. The

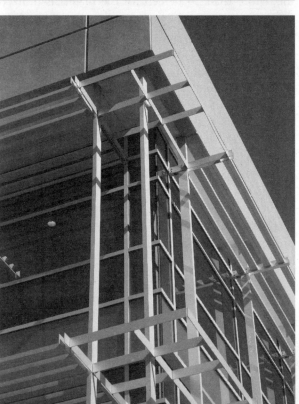

TOP LEFT: Efficient mechanical system, effected by light-harvesting, low-emissivity glazing, light sensors, and shading, optimize the building's energy performance.

TOP RIGHT: Entry foyer features locally sourced materials.

BOTTOM LEFT: Thermopane glass with low-E coating, deep sunshades, and sunscreens minimizes heat gain and helps maintain the thermal comfort of the occupants.

BOTTOM RIGHT: Exposed structural concrete with low-maintenance requirements is used throughout the building. Materials are local and employed in their natural state, not only blending in with their built and natural environment, but costing less than high-finish materials.

TOP: Ground level floor plan.

BOTTOM: Site plan.

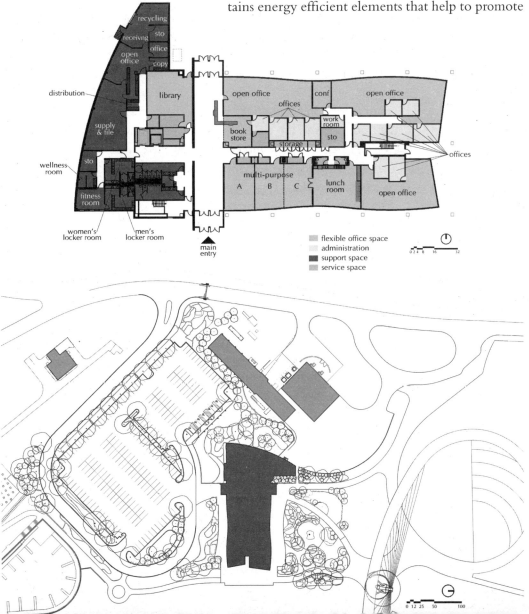

garden also teaches the public about the National Park Service's goals for sustainability. The bookstore and displays of the National Park Service's activities within the region, located in the building's lobby, also are accessible to the public.

This environmentally friendly building contains energy efficient elements that help to promote workers' well-being and productivity. The building's orientation offers river views for more than 90 percent of the interior workspaces. The same time, much of the building's interior is daylit. Due to the abundance of glazing, the lighting on the third floor is controlled with sensors to keep a constant preset brightness level, which adjusts to the daylight contribution. The use of controlled on/off sensors for areas within the first 15 feet of the exterior window on the first and second floors also allows for consistent light levels and helps to conserve energy.

Another important design consideration was the indoor air quality. The interior of the building uses raised flooring with underfloor air distribution, which decreases the buildup of carbon dioxide throughout the indoor environment. This method provides clean air close to occupants' workspaces instead of allowing contaminated air to come in from high above. This allows for better working conditions and a reduction of airborne illnesses.

Workers have a variety of options to commute to work, as the building design facilitates the use of alternative transportation. Employees may recharge their electric-powered vehicles using the power outlets located in the parking lot. The building features locker rooms and secure storage to make bicycle transportation a feasible option. In addition to the nearby biking trail, public transportation is readily available for workers and visitors.

Given a tight window of only 14 months to design and build, the design and construction team had to work very closely to achieve its aggressive goal of LEED Gold certification. Overall, employees and city officials are extremely pleased with the design and are proud of the certification.

INDOOR ENVIRONMENT

Upon entering the lobby of the Carl T. Curtis Midwest Regional Headquarters for the National Park Service, visitors will find an open, welcoming environment that embodies the philosophy of sustainability and provides a visual connection to the natural world. The lobby features many accents that express the National Park Service's care for the environment. The connection of the interior lobby to the outdoor environment is expressed through an arc pattern in the stained concrete floor, as well as the use of rough-cut Kansas limestone blade wall that intersects through the north-south axis of the lobby. Both elements, whose warm tones are dispersed throughout the facility, help to tie the inside and outside together.

Throughout the interior, occupants will find many building elements that were left in their natural, and sometimes unrefined, states while adding character to the space. Many of these elements incorporated a practice called *wabi-sabi,* a Japanese term meaning the aesthetic acceptance of a material with its natural imperfections, instead of being covered with the typical practice of studs and gypsum drywall. The predominant materials found inside are exposed cast-in-place concrete columns, beams, and underside floor slabs, as well as exposed roof decking. Most of these elements did not require any additional finishes such as stain or paint. The floor of the building's lobby is made with stained concrete instead of tile flooring, accepting the fact that natural cracks and shading of the floor will occur. Maple, which is native to many of the areas of the country that this regional headquarters serves, was used on doors and cabinets. The natural sugaring that occurs in the grain of maple was used with a clear finish, allowing its natural pattern to show through. Exposed steel beams, pendant-mounted light fixtures, and a few dropped ceilings complete the raw, industrial look of the interior.

The office areas feature an open layout designed for adaptable conditions. The majority of work spaces are located along the windows, with the executive offices, conference rooms, and storage facilities located on the interior core of the building. This allows all workers to have an exterior view, differing from the typical office layout where only executives have a view. The modular cubicles and raised floors accommodate changing technology demands and tenant needs. Additionally, modular carpet tiles over access flooring allow the owner and tenants to have access to mechanical, electrical, and communication systems with minimal effort. Also, locating most of the ductwork in the floor allowed the ceiling to be uncluttered with exposed ducts.

The restrooms maintain a natural look with the use of Kansas Tuxedo Gray limestone, with its naturally occurring fossils, for the countertops and porcelain tile for the floor. The design for toilets and locker rooms incorporates environmentally friendly features such as low-flow showerheads, waterless urinals, dual-flush toilets, low-flow lavatories, and lavatories with autosensors.

Design features that block air pollutants' entry into the building's interior spaces add to the healthy indoor atmosphere. Walk-off grilles located at the entries remove contaminants from occupants' shoes as they enter the building. Chemicals and pollutants present in the main copy center remain isolated in that room and are directly exhausted to the outside. Only chemicals that can be disposed of through the sanitation sewer lines are used in the building. Also, the design incorporated low-emission interior finishes, including paint, varnish, carpet, fabrics, wall coverings, sealants, and adhesives.

DAYLIGHTING

Large glass curtain walls provide most of the occupied space with daylight, in addition to 90 percent of all employees with views of the Missouri River, the bike trail system, and the teaching garden.

The abundant amount of natural lighting greatly contributes to the inviting feeling this facility possesses. The building sits on an east-west axis, which increases daylighting and provides most of the interior workspaces with access to exterior views of the landscape and the river. Glass bays and raised ceilings found throughout the building further provide a feeling of openness. On the first floor, the glass windows are shaped to mimic the movement of the river.

Large windows continue to surround the second and third levels. The building's top floor features five oversized glass bays and a raised ceiling to provide a vast quantity of natural light that retracts deep into the interior. Balconies facing the river also have been built to provide employees a place to gather while enjoying the outside. Even interior offices, including conference rooms, have sidelights to allow daylight and views to the outside. Furthermore, the building uses a light-harvesting technology with sensors that adjust the lighting based on a preset level. The sensors provide lighting according to available sunshine, allowing for a constant brightness level.

All of the artificial lighting can be controlled to increase comfort for the building's occupants while simultaneously saving energy. The high U-value glass used for the windows reduces the amount of incoming heat and harmful ultraviolet rays. The heavy massing and minimal windows in the west elevation block the intense afternoon sunlight, whereas on the east elevation, a combination of windows and walls prevent glare and solar heat gain from the early sun. Sun shades help block the summer sun while bouncing light deep into the open office areas.

WORLD BIRDING CENTER
MISSION, TEXAS

12

Completed: 2004

Owner: Texas Parks & Wildlife

Architects:
Lake Flato Architects
David Lake, FAIA
Bob Harris, AIA, LEED AP
Roy Schweers, Isabel Mijangos, Darryl Ohlenbusch, AIA
Margaret Sledge, Heather DeGrella, LEED AP

Consultants:
Halff Associates—Civil Engineering
Architectural Engineers Collaborative—Structural Engineering
Encotech Engineering Consultants—MEP Engineering
Kingscreek Landscaping—Landscape Design
Archillume Lighting Design—Lighting Design

General Contractor: SpawGlass

Photographer: Hester + Hardaway

Site: The site is dominated by two existing elements: the agricultural fields and the canal on their southern edge. The canal holds irrigation water pumped from the Rio Grande River. The fields contain the rich soil that once supported dense Tamaulipan thorn scrub. By situating the visitors center within the transition area between these linked elements we had an opportunity to interpret the story of a lost habitat while forming a gateway into the park's preservation area.

Environment: Rural—The World Birding Center is located along the Rio Grande in an area of Texas that is intensively farmed. The area is increasingly being defined by new housing subdivisions.

Program: Restoration of habitat is the primary focus of the visitor center grounds. For this reason the buildings are intended to simply play a background and support role. They enclose space for interior functions and facilitate

Essential to the design was creating comfortable exterior spaces that connected visitors with the wildlife habitats within the complex.

a comfortable interaction with the landscape gardens. Shady porches open up onto these gardens.

Square Footage: 13,000 square feet

Sustainable Features:
- Efficient program—original 20,000-square-foot program was right-sized to 13,000 square feet
- Passive solar design
- Passive ventilation
- Efficient structural design—48 percent less steel than traditional framing
- Extensive water conservation and reuse program
- Efficient systems—high-efficiency, variable speed mechanical equipment, on-demand water heaters, high-efficiency lighting
- Indigenous low-maintenance landscaping with flooded habitat demonstration
- Aluminum windows and louvers—75 percent recycled content aluminum frames with double-insulated high-efficiency glazing
- Concrete with 30 percent fly ash
- Sheathing—100 percent recycled content and radiant barrier
- Extensive use of salvaged, Forest Service–certified and/or engineered wood products

Structural System:
- Frame: bolted galvanized steel
- Floor: high fly ash content concrete
- Roof: highly efficient structural steel arch panels to form the shell roof system
- Partitions: reclaimed wood, regional clay block, high fly ash content concrete

Mechanical Systems:
- High-efficiency (min. SEER-15) variable speed air-conditioning units
- Fabric air ducts in exposed ceilings provide quiet operation and more even air distribution

Materials:
- Reclaimed cypress siding, regional clay block walls
- Galvanized, corrugated steel roofing
- Zero- to low-VOC content paints and sealants
- Local brick pavers, salvaged cypress flooring
- 100 percent recycled content formaldehyde-free MDF cabinetry, reused
- Salvaged cypress and natural mesquite benches

PROJECT DESIGN

Nourished by a mighty river and blessed with a semitropical climate, the Lower Rio Grande Valley at the southern tip of Texas has for a century nurtured commercial citrus groves and truck farms of onions, cabbage, lettuce, carrots, beets, and spinach. The borderland's agricultural economy has in turn engendered a random, low-tech approach to agrarian architecture. Over time, as needs arise, farmers add new buildings to augment field compounds of barns, garages, and warehouses. These seemingly haphazard accumulations of structures, varied in size and purpose, manifest a utilitarian vernacular that demonstrates a piecemeal response to the fluctuating fortunes of seasonal harvests.

This casual, gradual aesthetic influenced the project designer. The client, Texas Parks and Wildlife, wanted a new visitor center built within an existing state park that would attract birdwatchers from around the world. The client asked for a regionally appropriate design, which for many meant a Spanish colonial-style facility that would reflect the Hispanic heritage of the local built environment along this southernmost stretch of the U.S.-Mexico frontier. But as the designers crisscrossed the rural countryside they were struck by a completely different context, one that sprang from an agricultural vocabulary—clusters of buildings that would create quiet places in that landscape.

The wide span of the Quonset roof structure allowed for deep porches and unobstructed but protected views of bird and butterfly habitats.

Drawing upon this uncomplicated, utilitarian ethos, the architects designed a 13,000-square-foot complex of long and narrow structures that sits lightly on a 60-acre site along the Rio Grande adjacent to one of the last remaining unspoiled habitats in the valley. Three buildings oriented in an east-west direction contain administrative offices and a visitors center that serves birdwatchers who travel to this remote destination along North America's major migratory flyway.

The buildings are composed of a handful of simple materials with exposed structural members and Quonset-style corrugated metal arches. These roofs allow for 32-foot clear spans and also shelter exterior corridors. The buildings are connected by walkways paved with local brick and shaded from the relentless sunshine by flowering vines trained to go up galvanized metal arbors. Large cisterns harvest rainwater that is released periodically to flood a series of gardens set in between the buildings. The resulting shallow ponds are reminiscent of ox-bow lakes (or *resacas*) that the Rio Grande's intermittent floods used to create before upstream dams were built. These man-made water features attract hundreds of species of birds that feed off insects and the small marine creatures that inhabit the ponds. The complex comprises a microcosm of the region's ecosystems and corresponds with the natural world's material economy and sustainable design.

The headquarters was built parallel to an existing irrigation canal on a site that previously was a 60-acre onion field.

PROJECT CONSTRUCTION

The design team assembled a minimalist composition for the World Birding Center using a simple palette of materials—corrugated metal panels for roofing, fly ash concrete and recycled steel for structural framework, clay blocks, and salvaged cypress planks for cladding, aluminum and glass window wall infill.

While the construction of the three buildings might appear identical upon first glance, closer inspection reveals significant differences. The most obvious is the contrast in structural components.

Where the two buildings aligned on the north side of the complex use a lightweight matrix of steel pipe to support their roofs, the third building (running parallel but placed just to the south of the other two) employs thick concrete buttresses that give it a relatively greater sense of permanence. That building, specifically dedicated to exhibits, was designed to stand out as a destination point that would subtly draw the attention of the visiting birders.

In contrast to the exhibit wing's visual heft, the other two buildings evince a lighter framework of slender columns of steel pipe attached to horizontal steel members on which the barrel-vaulted roofs

LEFT: Ubiquitous to farm buildings throughout the countryside, corrugated metal respects the agricultural context of the region. The use of arched panels for the self-supporting roof allowed for a 48 percent reduction in steel by weight for the project.

RIGHT: The design called for spacious exterior porches to provide a buffer between indoors and outdoors.

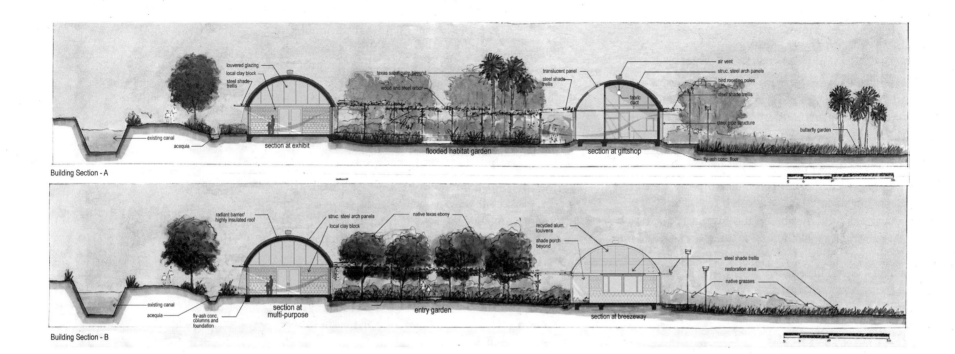

Building Section - A

Building Section - B

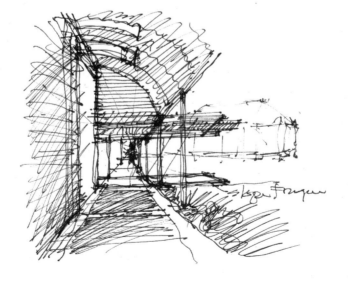

TOP: The architects intended for the buildings to be enveloped by the landscape so visitors would be immersed in their experience of nature.

BOTTOM: From the beginning of the design phase, the architects planned for generous overhang of the roof to shelter exterior corridors and bring visitors into close contact with wildlife habitats.

are set. With their structural components bolted together on-site, these buildings can be easily disassembled and reassembled should programmatic requirements change. The same design for maximum versatility is evident in the walkways that connect all the buildings, where steel pipes support horizontal shade structures and trellises for trained vines.

The foundations are grids of concrete formulated with a high percentage of fly ash, a by-product of coal-burning electric power plants. The open grid is inlaid with locally fabricated brick pavers—glazed units for interior spaces and unglazed for outdoors—set in a herringbone pattern. Natural clay blocks from D'Hanis (a small town about 250 miles north) in various sizes comprise most of the interior and exterior walls. More than just creating an efficient double-wall thermal envelope, the vitrified blocks are composed in an interesting stratified pattern that adds character and texture to the buildings' skin. On other walls that are protected from wind and rain by overhangs, the architects specified siding milled from "sinker" cypress logs salvaged from rivers and bayous along the Gulf coast.

The architect designed an observation deck called the Hawk Tower that is installed about a mile from the main facility. The structure's foundation utilizes helical piers that minimize the impact of more substantial structural elements. The piers are screwed into the ground and can be unscrewed later and used elsewhere, leaving little to no disturbance to the land.

PROJECT USE

The World Birding Center was designed to provide visitors with a memorable experience of being immersed in nature. As such, the complex offers many opportunities to observe environments created to attract migratory birds and other wildlife. The idea was to maintain the visitors' connection with the outdoors even while ensconced within the air-conditioned interior spaces.

This experience begins as visitors exit their vehicles in the adjacent parking lot and move through the first of a succession of outdoor gardens—the restoration of habitat is the primary intent of the landscaping. (In addition to the more than 500 species of birds that frequent the environs, the naturalists on the staff have identified several types of butterflies that were previously unknown to North America.)

A flooded garden was created within the complex. It is intended to mimic oxbow lakes created along the Rio Grande before dams were built to control the river upstream. Also known as *resacas,* these seasonal bodies of water formed when the river overflowed its banks. These lakes stood isolated for long periods of time, and birds would feed on stranded fish and small crustaceans such as crayfish and shrimp in these lakes. Water is periodically released from on-site cisterns (or pumped from an on-site well when no harvested rainwater is available) to flood the garden and jump-start the activity. Today, natural resacas are exceedingly rare due to man-made flood control measures.

Visitors can walk around this riparian ecosystem under the shaded walkways that connect the exhibits building and the entry wing, or they can linger on porches that open to the gardens. Or for those who choose to remain indoors, abundant use of high-performance insulated glass affords a comfortable perch for viewing an everchanging portrait of nature in the rough.

While the architecture is essential to the mission of the World Birding Center, the designers hoped that the structures would enhance rather than detract from the surrounding natural environment. "What we were interested in was more the place than the object, especially in a nature center like this," says Robert Harris, AIA, the project architect for Lake/Flato. "The experience is what's important, and the experience is going into nature. We want our building to fit into that experience in an elegant way, and support that experience. We want it to be unique and interesting and meaningful, and to immerse them in an environment in the way many visitors centers do not."

EFFICIENT USE OF SUSTAINABLE MATERIALS

The minimal environmental impact of the World Birding Center, including its construction and life cycle costs, represents a welcome change from the normal design and construction practices in the Lower Rio Grande Valley of southern Texas. Much to the credit of the Texas Parks and Wildlife Department, the state agency decided that the principles of green design would guide the development of the World Birding Center's headquarters.

The architects conceived a model for sustainable design that incorporated, among other things, local materials and highly efficient technical systems. From the outset, the design approach was to do *more* with *less*. Notably, the design team worked with the client to identify redundancies in programmatic space allotments and areas that could be designated for more flexible use. That led to an overall decrease in the project's square footage from 20,000 to 13,000, resulting in multiple savings.

Following are a number of examples that demonstrate how the design team maximized the efficiency of materials and systems used. The design of the Quonset hut roof used 48 percent less steel by weight in comparison to a steel truss roof. That translates directly into proportional reductions in use of raw materials extracted from the earth, energy impacts of the manufacturing process, and the first cost of the structure. Also, the panels' galvanized coating reflects heat and protects from corrosion. The decision to construct the self-supporting metal arch system with 2-foot by 8-foot corrugated roof panels also saved energy in their shipment to the site—fewer truck loads were required because the panels were nested together like spoons for transport. (Like the Quonset-style roof form, corrugated metal—as ubiquitous to the border region as pickup trucks—further connects the headquarters complex with its environmental and cultural context.) The concrete used for the foundations and for part of the structure is formulated with fly ash (a waste by-product produced by coal-fired power plants) as a replacement for the Portland cement normally used. Though fly ash makes very strong, lightweight concrete

The project's minimal use of durable materials, including board-formed concrete buttresses and natural clay block, underscores the simplicity of its design.

(it was used extensively in the Hoover Dam), it is not commonly used in concrete today—millions of tons are dumped in landfills annually.

Low-maintenance materials, such as galvanized steel that requires no paint, were a priority for the client due to the harsh climate conditions common to the southern Texas borderland. Other highly durable materials on the project include bare concrete, unfinished pavers, natural clay block masonry, and cypress siding that needs no sealant (which would rapidly break down under exposure to the constant sun and seasonally heavy rains). Exterior doors were fabricated from the same insect-resistant sinker cypress.

13

NATIONAL OUTDOOR LEADERSHIP SCHOOL HEADQUARTERS
LANDER, WYOMING

Completed:	2002
Owner:	National Outdoor Leadership School
Architects:	Centerbrook Architects and Planners
	James C. Childress, FAIA, Partner in Charge
	Thomas J. Lodge, AIA, Project Manager
	Jeffrey Gotta, R.A., Peggy V. Sullivan, AIA, Anita Macagno Cecchetto, AIA
	Susan J. Pinckney, ASID, Wendy B. Johnson, AIA
Consultants:	Inberg-Miller Engineers—Civil Engineers
	Gibble Norden Champion Brown—Structural Engineer
	The Ballard Group—Mechanical Engineers
	Innovative Electrical Systems, Inc.—Electrical Engineers
	P. R. Sherman, Inc.—Code Consultants
	Robert Schwartz and Associates—Specifications
	SE Group—Landscape Architect
	Rider Hunt Chartwell, LLC—Cost Consultant
General Contractor:	Kloetkorn-Ballard Construction/Development, Inc.
Photographer:	Jeff Goldberg/Esto
Site:	The headquarters is in downtown Lander, Wyoming, population 6,200. The site is a simple square parking lot bounded by a street and sidewalk on two sides, an alley on the third side, and an existing building on the fourth.

The unfinished steel leaf canopy is an icon for NOLS and provides protection for the stair egress at the rooftop garden.

Environment: Urban/rural—the project is located in "downtown" Lander, Wyoming. Lander, in turn, is located where the prairie meets the foothills of the Wind River Mountains.

Program: NOLS needed a new headquarters building that could accommodate all of their program, development, and admissions staff in one location. Offices, meeting rooms, and a variety of informal gathering places for visitors, students, faculty, and staff were requested. The building also needed to accommodate directors and staff from the national and international divisions who congregate in Lander on their off-seasons to develop programs and prepare for upcoming classes.

Square Footage: 51,520 square feet

Sustainable Features:
• Built on a vacant lot in an urban setting
• Built to age gracefully and last 100 years
• Building's orientation and narrow configuration maximize natural light
• Exterior sun shades, interior light shelves limit heat gain and maximize natural light
• 90 percent of materials manufactured within a 500-mile radius
• Recycled, sustainable, low-VOC interior materials used exclusively
• Natural ventilation through economizer cycle mechanical system
• Daylight harvested light fixtures; occupancy sensors also installed
• Dedicated trash and recycling management and storage
• Bike storage inside and outside; changing and shower rooms
• Rooftop garden
• Low-impact planting

Structural System:
- Steel frame
- Glulam floor and roof plates with concrete topping slab

Mechanical System:
- Variable air volume, gas-fired heating and cooling system.
- Economizer cycle provides free cooling and ventilation.

Materials:
- Brick made regionally from native sand
- Cast stone banding and window sills
- Exposed locally obtained aggregate walks
- Unfinished steel is used in leaf canopy, the sunshades, sloping slabs at entry, interior stairs, and trim
- Roof ballast excavated from site
- Glulam heavy timber
- Clear and transparent glazing partitions and doors
- Custom millwork and workstations; recycled content components and biocomposite panels
- Rubber flooring—recycled auto tires
- Carpet—recycled content
- Stained concrete stairs and floors
- Tectum ceilings—cementitious wood fiber acoustic panels
- Low-VOC paints
- Natural finish common American species wood trim—oak and fir
- Recycled wood flooring

Exterior and interior sun visors of unfinished steel provide shade from the strong western light and reflect light deep into the building.

PROJECT DESIGN

The National Outdoor Leadership School (NOLS) is one of the premier teachers of outdoor skills and leadership, offering wilderness courses throughout the world. As such, they wanted their new headquarters to embody their commitment to sustainable design, their sense of frugality, and their respect for the local community. In addition, they wanted a building with simple forms and finishes and as much natural light inside the building as possible. Finally, they wanted the building to be sensitive to the surrounding town context.

To design a building that has a local identity, the headquarters was designed through the use of collaborative workshops. This process brought together the users of the building (staff and faculty) with the design team (architects and engineers). The architects and engineers educated the users about the key issues to be considered and the users educated the design team about their needs, collectively establishing the goals for the building.

Once the key issues were identified and the goals established, seven or eight alternate solutions for the building were considered. These alternate schemes were used to balance the pros and cons of differ-

TOP LEFT & RIGHT: The central staircase of unfinished steel provides access to all floors and the rooftop garden.

BOTTOM: The column-free space in the open office wings allows flexible configuration. To the right are alcoves for individual offices and meeting areas. Sliding glass panels provide privacy and borrowed light between the two areas.

The tent-shaped central room provides a gathering place for students, visitors, and staff.

ent building configurations. The group considered which schemes worked best in plan, which was the most energy efficient, and which had the most appropriate image. Based on this evaluation the best ideas were collected and three or four more schemes were created for further evaluation. The process was repeated until a consensus was reached on the best balance of function, form, energy efficiency, and image. (For instance, it was determined a flat roof building provided better snow protection and a more appropriate image for NOLS and Lander).

It was also through this workshop process that sustainable strategies were evaluated. With "off-the-grid" facilities around the world, NOLS knows what systems work, which don't, and which are difficult to maintain. While special systems were evaluated, such as gray water irrigation, waterless urinals, photovoltaics, and pellet heating, this analysis led to simpler passive solutions for heating, cooling, and lighting. The focus was on systems that were maintainable, easy to care for, and appropriate for their environment. For instance, natural ventilation is achieved through mechanical means instead of operable windows due to the dusty location, and energy efficiency is achieved by maximizing the amount of natural light and reducing heat loss and gain through orientation and shading.

The workshop process allowed the design team to evaluate and balance the architectural, structural, and mechanical systems early in the design process. The process allowed energy efficient considerations to shape the building and optimized the systems to the Lander environment, leading to simpler and, in most cases, less expensive construction. In a sense, form followed sustainability.

During the design process it was determined that the largest single energy use for the building would be the artificial lighting. Solutions were sought that would maximize natural light throughout the interior and reduce the need for artificial light. The design team studied narrow buildings versus atrium buildings and balanced lighting costs against the costs for the heat loss and gain of different perimeter and volume configurations.

This analysis led to a U-shaped building—central block flanked by two office blocks. The office wings are only 45 feet wide and have 10-foot-high ceilings. The office wings are oriented north–south to capture softer east–west light and minimize harsh south light. The central wing, which does face south, contains a two-story gathering space that helps bring light deeper into this support wing. Open offices are on one side of each office wing, and alcoves for individual offices and meeting areas are on the other. Sliding glass panels provide privacy and borrowed light between the two areas.

The energy efficient solutions that proved the most viable, and financially effective, were simple passive ones adapted to local conditions. Materials and details were selected that would age gracefully and require minimal or no maintenance. The exterior is brick, similar in character to surrounding buildings. Precast bands form window sills and heads that reflect the thin rock banding found in the surrounding foothills. To reflect the nearby iron oxide Red Cliffs, unfinished steel is used throughout the building. The column-free space inside allows for flexible configurations. In addition, there are a minimum of hung ceilings and painted surfaces, and recycled materials were used whenever possible.

Exterior and interior sun visors on all windows provide shading of strong western light and reflect light deep into the building. Tinted glass helps control

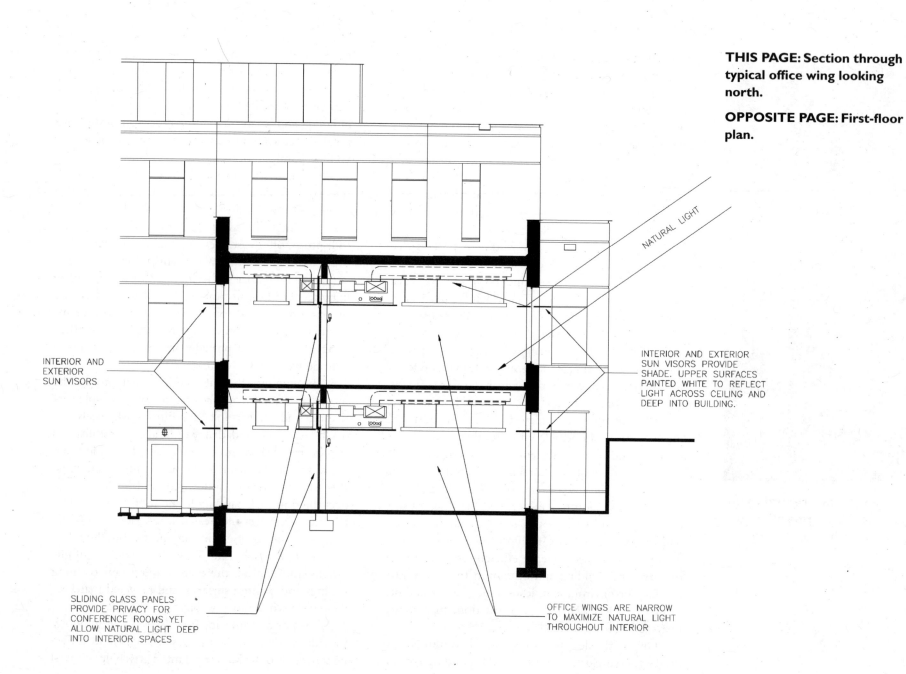

THIS PAGE: Section through typical office wing looking north.

OPPOSITE PAGE: First-floor plan.

NATURAL LIGHT

INTERIOR AND EXTERIOR SUN VISORS PROVIDE SHADE. UPPER SURFACES PAINTED WHITE TO REFLECT LIGHT ACROSS CEILING AND DEEP INTO BUILDING.

INTERIOR AND EXTERIOR SUN VISORS

SLIDING GLASS PANELS PROVIDE PRIVACY FOR CONFERENCE ROOMS YET ALLOW NATURAL LIGHT DEEP INTO INTERIOR SPACES

OFFICE WINGS ARE NARROW TO MAXIMIZE NATURAL LIGHT THROUGHOUT INTERIOR

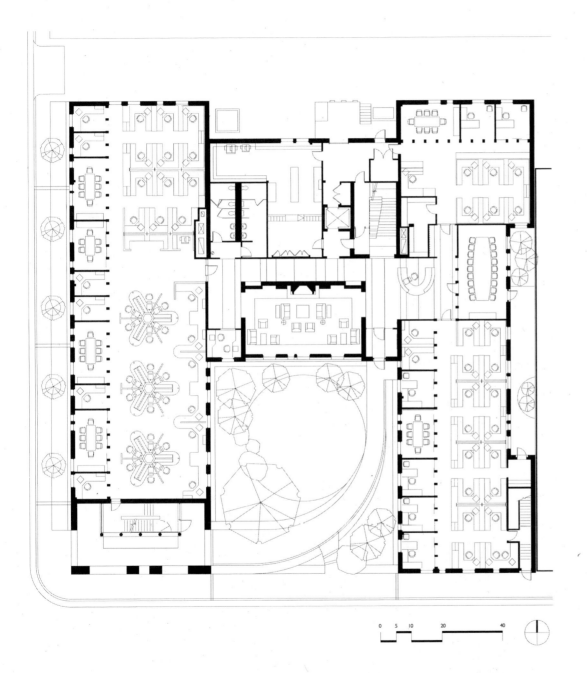

heat loss and gain. A Wyoming rooftop garden was installed to minimize heat loss and gain. The garden is made of river rock excavated from the site and steel planters filled with indigenous plants that do not require irrigation. The building's leaf canopy provides covered protection for an egress stair and shading for the rooftop garden. As an icon for NOLS, it is also a source of curiosity for the local community.

Natural ventilation is provided mechanically, as open windows are not practical due to the high winds, dust, and traffic noise. The heating and cooling system includes an economizer cycle to provide free cooling when possible.

PROJECT CONSTRUCTION

NOLS and Centerbrook selected a contractor early in the design process. This gave the team the benefit of the contractor's input early on. The collaboration between owner, design team, and contractor helped ensure practical solutions to design issues. It also helped make the contractor sensitive to the environmental issues that needed to be taken into consideration when constructing the building.

The contractor was a valuable resource in finding locally made products that would meet the budget. Normal balancing of the mechanical systems was completed but it was decided not to commission the building due to the additional cost—a cost that is difficult to justify on small projects, especially for nonprofit organizations. In hindsight, commissioning may have helped prevent a problem the heating system has in responding quickly to an extreme drop in temperature, a periodic occurrence in Lander.

PROJECT USE

The NOLS Headquarters met and exceeded the expectations of the client and its staff. The building demonstrates in a tangible way NOLS' core values of community and sensitivity to protecting the environment summarized as "Leave No Trace." The headquarters building is a physical manifestation of NOLS' mission statement. Short of providing additional space, this has been one of the building's greatest contributions to the organization. At the outset of the process, NOLS did not fully anticipate the impact the building would have on the visitors and the staff.

As the most prominent building in Lander, the building shows NOLS' commitment to the community and has become a Wyoming meeting place for external groups of all kinds. When visiting the headquarters, visitors sense NOLS is who they say they are.

The staff has had a very positive response to working in the building. This is due to its character with natural light and "sun energy" everywhere. The building is very effective at encouraging interaction, whether it be one-on-one or in large groups. The open office areas allow informal meetings and conversations among staff while the meeting rooms and alcoves provide alternate places for both scheduled and impromptu gatherings.

People in the local community tend to think of sustainability as recycling and walking to work, or energy systems that are visible, such as photovoltaic cells. Given that the NOLS building's sustainable aspects are passive and nontechnical in nature, and therefore subtle, the staff strives to educate people about the specific strategies used throughout the building. Nevertheless, the headquarters does convey an overall impression that NOLS and its staff are concerned about sustainability and that they are doing something about it.

While the budget included additional money for both more durable and more sustainable materials, the economic trade-offs of minimal maintenance costs for the shell of the building have started to take effect. The extensive daylighting scheme has proven to be very effective, not only in reducing artificial lighting costs but in the overall quality of life in the building.

TOP: The square entry courtyard is an informal gathering place and is also used for orientation meetings with new students. The garden is made of river rock excavated from the site and unfinished steel planters filled with indigenous plants.

BOTTOM: The Wyoming rooftop garden provides dramatic views. The leaf canopy provides protection for the staircase and shade for the garden.

NOLS is a founding partner of the "Leave No Trace" Center for Outdoor Ethics and runs the program's master educator courses. The national program is dedicated to promoting and inspiring responsible recreational practices. It is a partnership of federal land management agencies, outdoor educators, conservation groups, manufacturers, outdoor retailers, user groups, and individuals who share a commitment to preserving and protecting our public lands.

As NOLS developed plans for a new headquarters building, they wanted the "Leave No Trace" principles of respect for the environment to be incorporated into the design of their new building. This led to a number of design decisions. NOLS wanted a headquarters with the lightest impact possible on the environment. The first decision they made was to remain in downtown Lander rather than build on open land, despite the cost premium to stay in town. As the largest employer in Lander, NOLS believed the most socially conscious choice was to remain there and contribute to its vitality and leave rural property pristine.

NOLS then invested in a building they hope will endure because the systems are simple, the plan is adaptable, and the materials are detailed to last 100 years or more. This long-term perspective was achieved by balancing up-front costs, life cycle costs, and maintenance/operating costs. NOLS opted to spend additional money on durable materials that would need minimal or no maintenance and that would age gracefully. The building's flexible, largely column-free space, allows easy reconfigurations for the future.

Finally, this approach figured prominently in the process of material selection for the building. Both the client and the design team looked carefully for locally sourced, recycled, and durable materials. Building materials included glulam heavy timbers, custom millwork, workstations made of recycled content components and biocomposites, rubber flooring from recycled auto tires, brick made regionally from native sand, locally obtained exposed aggregate walks, and roof ballast excavated from the site. Recycled, sustainable, low-VOC materials were used exclusively for interior materials.

Downtown Lander, Wyoming with Wind River Mountains beyond

ISLANDWOOD
BAINBRIDGE ISLAND, WASHINGTON

Completed:	2002
Owner:	IslandWood
Architects:	Mithun
	Bert Gregory, AIA, Principal
	Richard Franko, AIA, Project Manager
	David W. Goldberg, AIA, Project Designer
	Lynn Robbins; Tom Rooks; Amanda Sturgeon; Christoph Kruger, AIA;
	Brian Cloward; Susan McNabb; John Harrison, AIA; Daniel Swaab;
	Ken Pirie; Chris Dixon, RS, CCS; Tom Johanson; Konning Tam;
	Serge Martin
Interior Design:	Elizabeth MacPherson, IIDA, ASID; Cindy Schmidt; Lisa Herriot, IIDA
Consultants:	Browne Engineering—Civil
	Skilling, Ward, Magnusson, Barkshire—Structural
	Keen Engineers—Mechanical
	Cross Engineers—Electrical
	The Berger Partnership—Landscape and Planning
	William Isley—Master Planning Team
	David Rousseau, Archemy Consulting—Environmental Consulting
	2020 Engineers—Alternative Water Systems
	Mike Nelson, Washington St., Schott Applied Power—Photovoltaics
	Heliodyne—Solar Hot Water
	Sahale—Suspension Bridge Design
General Contractor:	Rafn Company: Educational Core
	Drury Construction: Art Studio & Site Structures
	Woodside Construction: Staff Housing
Photographer:	Roger Williams
	Doug Scott
	Dave Goldberg
	Art Grice

Roofs direct precipitation to cisterns for irrigation and boot washing.

Site:	A 70,000-square-foot campus located on 255 acres on Bainbridge Island comprising a nearly complete watershed as well as a bog, pond, cattail marsh, ravine, and multiple generations of logged forest.
Environment:	Rural
Program:	Forty buildings and site structures provide varied opportunities for experiential-based learning. Four thousand school children spend three nights at IslandWood exploring the site with naturalists on a series of linked pedestrian trails.
Square Footage:	70,000 square feet
Sustainable Features:	• No air-conditioning—windows open and buildings breathe. Students operate building controls and monitor their energy and water use during their stay. • The Living Machine® serves as a biological wastewater treatment plant and interactive aquatic science classroom. • Educational geological fireplaces, rainwater cisterns, and artist-made building parts facilitate an understanding of ecological connections and interactive hands-on learning. • Buildings are sited at the north edge of solar meadows, allowing solar access from the south and framed views deep into the forest beyond. • Natural entry trails provide a "decompression zone" for all visitors. Students work together to pull their bags in carts down a long rustic trail to their lodges. • Open-air site structures provide a dry place in the damp Northwest forest for writing, drawing, and outdoor field experiments. • As one of the first LEED Gold-certified projects in the country, IslandWood's campus and buildings serve as active participants in the teaching process.
Structural System:	• Butterfly roof
Mechanical System:	• Natural ventilation/no air-conditioning
Materials:	• Locally sourced, sustainable

PROJECT DESIGN

IslandWood, located on Bainbridge Island, is a 255-acre environmental education center. It is a place for urban schoolchildren to immerse themselves in nature: its sights, smells and sounds. Its immersive four-day teaching program creates a "School in the Woods" that bridges the gap between traditional education and the natural world, bringing ecology into the classroom and the classroom outside.

Children were integral to the design. They were one of the two "client" groups designated by the staff—the other client being the site itself. The project began with a green visioning charrette that included local schoolchildren, community members, teachers, and designers. Following these charrettes, landscape architects and planners performed detailed site and resource analyses to locate campus buildings with minimal impact, preserving mature forests and wetlands. All worked together with experts in ecology who offered design advice throughout its development. As a complement to the charrettes and ongoing research, designers camped out on-site to gain personal experience.

The architects, with an engineering and consultant team, worked with the IslandWood staff and the general contractor to fulfill the client's vision. This collaborative team produced Washington State's first LEED Gold-level certification.

While the complex contains 39 buildings and exterior structures, the welcome center, the dining hall, and the learning studios form the core of the campus. They also create a place that's well suited to the educational purpose it serves while retaining the whimsy of childhood. Every aspect of the project represents an opportunity for education. For example, the design team made a substantial commitment to using recycled or reclaimed materials on the project. Most of the wood was either reclaimed or harvested on-site and locally milled. The concrete uses fly ash in lieu of Portland cement. To highlight this, each of the classrooms features a different floor covering (bamboo, cork, recycled rubber, and so on) and a different countertop (sunflower hulls, soybean seeds, and others). Wherever there is a sustainable element in the project, there is a "way in" for the children. Perhaps the most vivid example of this approach of using the building as a learning tool is the Living Machine®—a hands-on water treatment system.

PROJECT CONSTRUCTION

At IslandWood, many decisions were made to protect and preserve the site while recognizing its unique teaching abilities. The site nearly encompasses a complete watershed that includes wetlands, a pond, and a stream, leaving water protected and filtered by these natural systems. Though the existing forest on the site was previously logged for years, it, too, was catalogued to ensure the oldest and largest trees

Students walking to the dining room.

THIS PAGE

TOP LEFT: Lodge detail at gable end.

TOP RIGHT: Main entry sequence.

BOTTOM LEFT: Main center reception.

BOTTOM RIGHT: Lodge window detail.

OPPOSITE PAGE

LEFT: Art studio exterior.

RIGHT: Great room fireplace highlighting local stones.

were saved during construction. Those trees that were removed were used for mulch or locally milled for the buildings' siding and trim. And all landscape comprises native northwest species requiring no irrigation beyond initial planting and establishment, encouraging animal habitat and students' exploration. One result of these endeavors is that only six acres out of the 255-acre site were developed.

All IslandWood buildings are designed to be built with easily reused or recycled materials that require little maintenance. Spaces are designed for multiple uses to allow for maximum flexibility over time; lodge bedrooms feature bunk beds for children's programs during the week and queen-sized Murphy beds for adults or families on weekends. Wood structures contain high fly ash content concrete stem walls. Forest Stewardship Council–certified lumber and glu-lam trusses are bolted together with recyclable steel connections. Materials are left unfinished and in a natural state, eliminating typical maintenance routines like painting, replacing carpeting, and repairing drywall. In-floor radiant heating combined with natural ventilation eliminates ductwork, reducing maintenance and improving air quality. The natural ventilation of the building was optimized using the Thermal Analysis System.

In addition to these large sustainable features, the design also features a series of small, tactile details to spur the children's curiosity. In keeping with the site's features and the school's mission, local craftspeople and artists created the furniture and artwork featured throughout IslandWood. From custom copper sinks with salmon motifs that alert users to the importance of water to multilayer stone fireplaces that tell the region's geologic history, these pieces help to edu-

cate, create a sense of place, and connect the buildings to the site.

PROJECT USE

IslandWood is designed for urban schoolchildren who wouldn't otherwise be immersed in the outdoors. It is meant to introduce these kids to the world beyond their neighborhoods and instill in them an appreciation for nature.

Students see their impact on the environment throughout their stay. They monitor their water and energy use through an integrated computer data network. They watch as their food waste is composted and used for organic gardening, and they watch as rainwater irrigates vegetables that they will eat.

In support of this integrated sustainable agenda, most visitors to the site arrive by bus or ferry. Drivers are encouraged to carpool. Alternative fueling is provided for propane vehicles, while bike storage and shower facilities encourage alternative means for those who work at IslandWood.

All building wastewater is treated on-site to tertiary standards using a Living Machine® and Subsurface Flow Constructed Wetlands. Water from the Living Machine® is reused for toilet flushing at the dining hall and main center bathrooms. Rainwater is collected from building roofs into concrete cisterns for irrigation and boot washing. In the administration area, open offices allow for flexibility and strong team collaboration. Natural wood blinds, retractable canopies, and mechanized skylight blinds control daylight.

ABOVE: Fossils inlaid into the stonework.

OPPOSITE: 70,000-square-foot campus on 255 acres of Bainbridge Island.

EDUCATION AND WATER CONSERVATION

IslandWood, on Bainbridge Island in Washington State, is intricately tied to water, offering a rich educational experience that teaches children about every facet of ecology, but especially the regional importance of water.

Surrounded by the water of Puget Sound, all life on the island, including human life, is dependent on its continued vitality. The Puget Sound has substantially influenced the area's rich and diverse forests and wildlife, and provides vital habitat for many marine animals including countless fish species, harbor seals, and majestic orcas. It is also an important stop for salmon on their journey to the open ocean.

IslandWood further encompasses one of Bainbridge Island's several vital watersheds that supply not only fresh water for the island's human inhabitants, but also a pristine habitat for indigenous plants and animals. These streams, wetlands, ponds, and subsurface aquifers are the lifeblood of the island, making it livable for a diverse array of plants, animals, and growing human communities.

In order to live up to its educational and environmental standards, IslandWood was built with three main water goals: water conservation, treatment and reclamation, and education. To reach these goals, IslandWood required a high level of transparency. Rather than simply meeting sustainability objectives behind the scenes, conservation and water treatment strategies were made visible and interactive. Instead of passively using water resources, students are able to see the entire water cycle and become active participants in its treatment and conservation. In short, students are made aware of their own impact on the environment and learn how to minimize it. The importance of water conservation is emphasized throughout the site. Even bathrooms educate with custom copper sinks featuring salmon motifs designed to promote the importance of water in the Pacific Northwest.

Because there are different forms of sustainable water treatment, two different systems were employed on-site for educational purposes. The first and more expensive system is the Living Machine®. The second and less expensive water treatment system works through Subsurface Flow Constructed Wetlands.

Located in the site's greenhouse, The Living Machine® is a compact wastewater treatment plant that produces tertiary level results. Drawing on a combination of filtration, oxygenation, and phytoplankton treatment, the system treats wastewater through an entirely organic process—without the use of harmful chemicals. Not only does the Living Machine® treat water, it also conserves it: water treated by the system is reused for toilet flushing in the dining hall and main center bathrooms. Because of the Living Machine's® compact size and accessible location, students can witness the treatment process firsthand, making it an ideal learning tool.

Wastewater from IslandWood's three lodges is treated with Subsurface Flow Constructed Wetlands (SFCW). These organic structures provide a high standard of water treatment with a lower price tag. The Constructed Wetlands are comprised of a gravel surface lined with cells of indigenous wetland plants that filter and treat the wastewater as it passes through and over them, providing unbeatable septic treatment while preserving the high water quality of area. While not as compact or centrally located as the Living Machine®, the SFCW still provides a highly visible form of green water treatment that can also easily be showcased for educational purposes.

Additional strategies were employed on-site to reuse and conserve water. Roofs were designed to capture rainwater, directing it to cisterns for irrigation and boot washing. The dining hall, the learning center, and the lodges all benefit from recycled rainwater. Composting toilets and waterless urinals are employed wherever possible, reducing potable water use in the main center, dining hall, and learning studios by 36 percent annually. In the future as funding becomes available, the visitor lodges will be plumbed for gray water reuse. All buildings

**Mechanical system
diagram.**

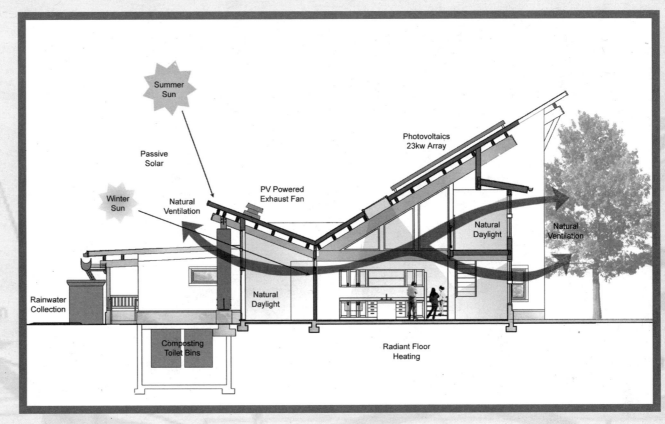

Summer
Sun

Passive
Solar

Winter
Sun

Natural
Ventilation

PV Powered
Exhaust Fan

Photovoltaics
23kw Array

Natural
Daylight

Natural
Ventilation

Rainwater
Collection

Natural
Daylight

Composting
Toilet Bins

Radiant Floor
Heating

and irrigation systems are designed to maintain the site's natural, pre-development stormwater patterns.

In order to reduce water use and preserve the natural qualities of the site, all new landscape is comprised of native species requiring no irrigation after plant establishment. The greenhouse and exterior garden allow for the growth of native plantings for replacement of invasive species. Children learn about the important role of plants in a watershed through direct involvement with the greenhouse and the planting process.

The earth and its inhabitants face many challenges in the coming decades. As the human population grows, freshwater sources will become more depleted and increasingly polluted. The overall effects of climate change remain to be seen, but the warming of the earth will certainly produce new problems like rising oceanic waters and severe inland droughts. People must therefore rise to the challenge of intelligent water use. By offering highly visible, hands-on educational opportunities, Island-Wood provides the next generation with firsthand knowledge about sustainable solutions for conserving, treating, and reclaiming water.

THE JOE SERNA, JR.— CALIFORNIA ENVIRONMENTAL PROTECTION AGENCY (CALEPA) HEADQUARTERS BUILDING

15

SACRAMENTO, CALIFORNIA

Completed:	December 2000
Owner:	City of Sacramento
Developer:	Thomas Properties Group
Architect/Design:	AC Martin Partners, Inc.
	Christopher C. Martin, Partner-in-Charge
	David Martin, FAIA, Principal Designer
	Carey McLeod, Principal-in-Charge
Consultants:	AC Martin Partners, Inc.—Civil Engineering
	CBM Engineers—Structural Engineering
	Levine/Seegel Associates—Mechanical Engineering
General Contractor:	Turner Construction
Photographer:	David Wakely
Site:	Strategically located city-owned site in downtown Sacramento's revitalization district near public mass transit.
Environment:	Urban (Downtown Sacramento)
Program:	After listening to the City of Sacramento, CalEPA, and the state's Department of General Services (DGS), the program that AC Martin Partners distilled from all was to create a new kind of integrated downtown office building, one that is innovative in a range of areas: environmental and green, designed and constructed in the most cost-effective way, supporting the urban context of the downtown area, and adding value to the lives of users and visitors.

Ground-floor entryway uses materials native to California.

Square Footage:	950,000 square feet
Sustainable Features:	• Tower oriented north–south
	• Energy efficient LED lighting (exterior roof lighting)
	• UV reflective modular precast panels
	• Solar shade overhangs
	• High-performance glass
	• Recycled and renewable materials used throughout xeriscaped entryway
	• High-efficiency variable sized chillers (basement)
	• Rooftop photovoltaic cells
	• Strategically located HVAC fans (pump fresh air into building)
	• High wall zone integrates with asymmetrical core for tenant flexibility
	• Low wall zone around perimeter places majority close to natural light
Structural System:	• Moment resistive steel frame with precast concrete panels (exterior cladding)
Mechanical System:	• Heating and cooling units were sized and located strategically throughout the building to optimize energy savings by using fresh air. The HVAC system was designed to feed 100 percent fresh air whenever possible to each floor of the building, improving both indoor air quality and energy efficiency. State of the art controls make use of cooler night air during early morning hours. The entire system saves up to 40 percent more energy than the most stringent building standards now in effect.
	• Conventional office buildings have one or two large chillers. This building has three of varying sizes. The smaller ones are used at night and weekends when demand is low. The result is significant life cycle savings.
Materials:	• Granite base, precast concrete panels, aluminum, glass curtain walls and aluminum louvers (at mechanical rooms)
	• Lobby space—glass, aluminum, and eucalyptus wood (renewable material)
	• Overall, building materials and furnishings were selected based on their established standards for low- or no-VOC, recycled content, ability to be recycled, embodied energy, and location of manufacturing facilities.
	• Recycled materials are incorporated into the design through the selection of carpet, acoustic panels, auditorium seats, cubicle surfaces, signage, and dozens of other components and furnishings with high recycled content throughout the building.

One hundred light-emitting diodes illuminate the CalEPA's top six floors.

Main center reception.

Students walking to the dining room.

15 THE JOE SERNA, JR.—CALIFORNIA ENVIRONMENTAL PROTECTION AGENCY (CALEPA) HEADQUARTERS BUILDING

SACRAMENTO, CALIFORNIA

Public art decorates interior and exterior areas.

The building is placed on-site to take advantage of maximum daylight.

The entry to the Thoreau Center for Sustainability (renovated historic Letterman Hospital) features the judicious insertion of new materials.

Corridor view.

17 THE ROBERT REDFORD BUILDING FOR THE NATURAL RESOURCES DEFENSE COUNCIL
SANTA MONICA, CALIFORNIA

Second-floor light well.

Main entrance to the Environmental Action
Center.

The entry highlights the palette of local woods.

View west.

Detail of exterior facade.

Internal view of the library, showing clerestory lighting scheme.

The building's design is intrinsic with nature.

The interior atrium serves as a climate buffer.

PROJECT DESIGN

"Designing a new kind of office building" was the central idea in the minds of the architect/design team. Conservation of energy resources and the economically viable use of recycled materials were prime considerations in the development of the project. In order to remain consistent with CalEPA's mission statement and to meet the needs of the community, a highly sustainable, design-sensitive building was realized.

Many factors influenced the design of the building, including budget and numerous city ordinances that worked against the project at times. Ultimately, the project was designed to respond to the user and optimize the limitations. The site was selected in the heart of downtown Sacramento, near public transportation and a historic park plaza. The L-shaped design of the building allowed for the creation of a transitional green space that created a dialogue with the city core. Placement on the site, massing, materials, public art, landscaping, and user-friendly amenities all combined to create one of the most integrated and sophisticated downtown office buildings in the country.

Design-build was selected as the delivery method, which resulted in a unique collaboration between developer, architect/designer, contractor, owner, and user. Early on in the predesign phase, a project management plan was developed to establish performance parameters. The plan clearly defined the project's

The building is placed on-site to take advantage of maximum daylight.

goal, objectives, and procedures, and covered subjects such as schedule and cost control, quality control, and design and construction phase procedures. The plan was structured so that additions and changes could be easily integrated as the project progressed. This fluid method allowed AC Martin Partners (ACMP) to integrate sustainable design elements that were not part of the original five-year budget.

PROJECT CONSTRUCTION

The level of collaboration and cooperation achieved among the project team members and various stake-holders was key to the success of the project. Early in the project the team participated in a partnering workshop to develop vision and mission statements. Team roles and responsibilities were defined as well as the sequence of required activities to complete the building on schedule. Biweekly team meetings were conducted to proactively address issues.

The project team includes a state agency leasing space through another public agency in a building owned by a third public agency that hired a private developer to oversee the design and construction of the building. The complexities of these relationships challenged the parties through all phases of the project. Clear vision and a design-build delivery process proved to be the keys to success.

The developer held numerous design consultant contracts and the general construction contract. Because of the fast track nature of design-build, the contractor was able to manage various bid packages proactively and obtain over 50 permits to meet the tight design and construction schedule. The design

phase was divided into distinct steps—schematic, design development, 50 percent construction documents, 100 percent construction documents, bid documents—for better quality and ultimately better budget control.

The original lease schedule called for full tenant occupancy in August 2001. The project was delivered in December 2000, eight months ahead of the original schedule. The city also saved several million dollars in incentive fees. The design-build method allowed for early fixed-cost commitments that minimized cost overruns, took advantage of favorable construction market conditions resulting in competitive subtrade bid prices, and expedited delivery as construction started before the design was complete. This was crucial because the green elements were not part of the original five-year budget. The design-build model afforded the project team the flexibility to work within the budget constraints, meet the demands of the client by integrating energy efficient design strategies into the process, and complete the project on schedule.

PROJECT USE

The new Joe Serna, Jr.—CalEPA Headquarters office building has transformed the downtown civic core and has become the new landmark in the City

LEFT: The lobby features a wide array of renewable material, including eucalyptus wood paneling.

RIGHT: Public art decorates interior and exterior areas.

of Sacramento. Visitors and downtown office workers now have a wonderful space in which to gather or relax. The courtyard and plaza of the project incorporates extensive public art and landscaping. Regional and internationally known artists were selected to create works of art that are based on the environmental themes located inside and outside the building. The developer also invested a million dollars to renovate the adjacent park and turn it into the classic "town square" located directly in front of the City Hall and diagonally from the project site. Taxpayers are benefited because efficiency of governmental operations was increased through the consolidation of scattered public employees.

After close to a year of occupancy, the building has become a model project in terms of energy efficiency and exceeds California's Building Energy Efficiency Standards requirements, also known as Title 24, by 36 percent. At the same time, employees enjoy a healthy environment with over 90 percent of the employees expressing satisfaction in the building's friendly systems and materials, its image and prestige, and the appearance of the grounds and courtyard.

The integrated approach taken by the designers allowed the building to be more than just another office building; it has solidified people's perceptions of sustainability. The building has become a transformational, sustainable, user-driven, enduring, and flexible landmark that owes its existence to the collaborative efforts of the core project team. These efforts, physically manifested in the design, construction, and use of the building, have allowed the building to garner the LEED Platinum EB certification, BOMA Toby Earth Award and Energy Star Award, and the 2002 DBIA's Design-Build Excellence Award.

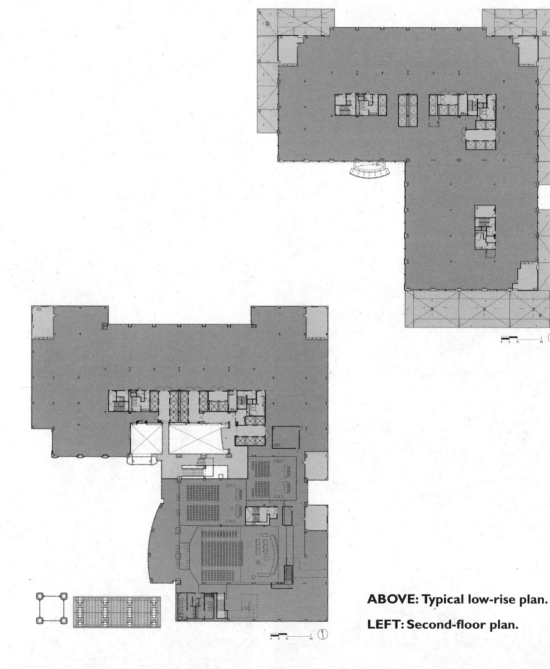

ABOVE: Typical low-rise plan.

LEFT: Second-floor plan.

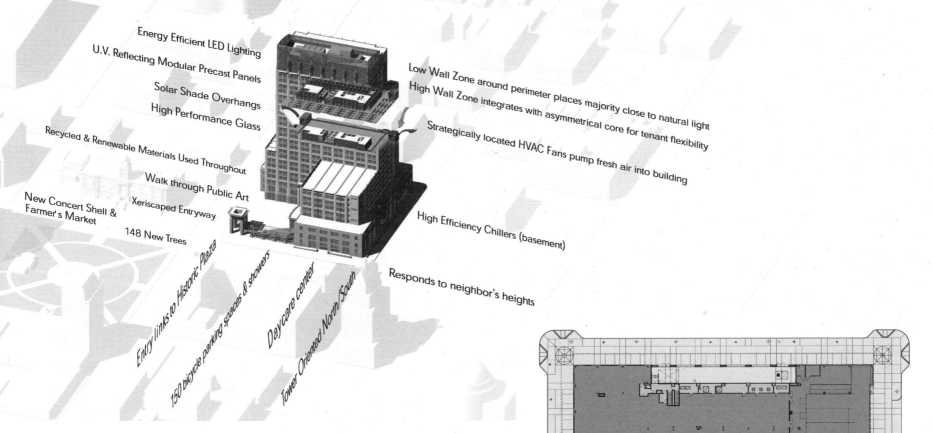

Energy Efficient LED Lighting

U.V. Reflecting Modular Precast Panels

Solar Shade Overhangs

High Performance Glass

Recycled & Renewable Materials Used Throughout

Walk through Public Art

New Concert Shell & Farmer's Market

Xeriscaped Entryway

148 New Trees

Low Wall Zone around perimeter places majority close to natural light

High Wall Zone integrates with asymmetrical core for tenant flexibility

Strategically located HVAC Fans pump fresh air into building

High Efficiency Chillers (basement)

Responds to neighbor's heights

Entry links to Historic Plaza

150 bicycle parking spaces & showers

Daycare center

Tower Oriented North/South

ABOVE: Schematic illustrating key design features of the building.

RIGHT: Ground-floor plan.

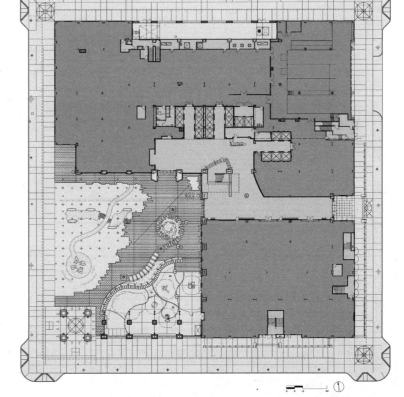

The xeriscaped plaza
entryway needs little or
no maintenance.

The mandate from the California State Governor's Office was "... deliver the most energy efficient and sustainable building on time and within budget—a showcase public building consistent with the organization's mission to preserve and protect the environment."

The response was a 25-story, 930,000-square-foot LEED EB Platinum building occupied by the California Environmental Protection Agency (CalEPA) that encompasses a city block and was the main effort of that agency's consolidation project. The project brought together approximately 3,000 employees together under one roof (from almost a dozen locations) for efficiency of operations and future growth. The project was programmed, designed, and constructed in 30 months with a construction budget of $115.7 million.

The design-build model facilitated the project team's ability to enhance sustainable building features while working within the budget constraints. The design is energy efficient and exceeds California's Title 24 energy model by approximately 36 percent; this was accomplished through building orientation, sun shading, energy efficient glass, daylighting, and air economizer HVAC systems. Photovoltaic cells on the south-facing rooftop provide renewable power, lowering the building's overall electrical consumption and preventing 3.2 million pounds of carbon monoxide and 35,000 pounds of sulfur and nitrogen oxide from entering the environment.

When the project commenced in the late 1990s, there were neither clearly stated user/owner requirements for energy efficiency nor State of California initiatives for sustainable design. USGBC's LEED scoring system was in its infancy and not part of the project, but ACMP knew that if the building were to be successful and foster the tenants of the CalEPA, the building would have to be made green through design innovation and a creative collaboration with the general contractor.

From the inception, choices were made at crucial times during design and construction to cultivate a greening of the building process. The building utilizes energy efficient glass and precast concrete panels as the exterior skin, architectural shading devices, and renewable materials such as the eucalyptus paneling throughout the building's lobby. Materials were selected for efficiency along with cost, longevity, and aesthetics. While sourcing sustainable materials can often be challenging and time-consuming, the shared experience and collaborative nature of the design/build team made this task much easier.

The building responds to the climate by its placement on the site and is aligned to take advantage of sunlight. HVAC systems were sized and located strategically throughout the building to optimize energy savings by using "free" fresh air. The HVAC system was designed to feed 100 percent fresh air whenever possible to each floor of the building, improving both indoor air quality and energy efficiency. State of the art controls make use of cooler night air during early morning hours. The entire system saves up to 40 percent more energy than the most stringent building standards now in effect. Once again the design-build structure of the team allowed for the designers, the engineers, and the subcontractors to understand this unique approach early enough in the process to flush out any issues before construction began.

While the building cost was competitive with other office buildings of similar size and occupancy, it has since seen a saving in excess of one million dollars per year for energy (electricity and gas). This project has demonstrated how creative choices make green buildings feasible. In fact, the sustainable design approach and results gathered from the CalEPA Headquarters building are validating Governor Schwarzennegger's current statewide initiative for green buildings.

THE THOREAU CENTER FOR SUSTAINABILITY
SAN FRANCISCO, CALIFORNIA

Completion date:	1996 (Phase I); 1998 (Phase II)
Architecture Firm:	Leddy Maytum Stacy Architects
Owner (Land):	National Park Service
Master Tenant:	Thoreau Center for Sustainability
Design Team:	• Developer: Equity Community Builders and the Thoreau Center Partners • Contractors: Plant Construction (Phase I), Herrero (Phase II) • Architect: Marsha Maytum, FAIA Principal-in-Charge, Charlie Stott, Project Architect • Structural: Steve Tipping and Associates • MEP: Flack and Kurtz • Lighting Design: Architectural Lighting Design • Landscape Design: Office of Cheryl Barton • Acoustic: Charles Salter Associates • Sustainable Material Consultant: Lynn Simon and Associates
Photographer:	Richard Barnes
Site:	The Historic Letterman Hospital in the Presidio National Park, a reserve of 1,480 acres at the edge of the San Francisco peninsula near the Golden Gate Bridge
Environment:	Urban/National Park
Program:	The 112,000-square-foot complex of historic structures was to be transformed into new offices, and public exhibition space for a nonprofit center of over 50 organizations working for social justice, community education and development, public health, and environmental stewardship. A primary project goal was for the Thoreau Center to become a national model for the successful integration of sustainable design practices and adaptive reuse for other military bases throughout the United States.

The entry to the Thoreau Center for Sustainability (renovated historic Letterman Hospital) features the judicious insertion of new materials.

Square Footage:	112,000 square feet (phases I and II)
Sustainable Features:	• Reuse of existing historic structures with minimal intrusion, demolition, and waste. Existing spaces were thoughtfully reused by matching client program to existing spaces. Contractor was required to report on amounts of waste removed and recycled. • Photovoltaic panels (Building 1016 entry) • Cotton insulation in walls • Sustainably harvested wood paneling for custom-designed workstations and wall panels • Recycled aluminum storefront at interior offices and exterior Porte cocheres • Bathroom tiles made from recycled windshields from cars and airplanes • Formaldehyde free paints • Naturally ventilated (cross-ventilated) office spaces taking advantage of the existing narrow office wings, operable windows, and attic roof vents. Open office plan allows air to circulate naturally. • High-efficiency hydronic heating control system • High-efficiency lighting and maximized daylighting through use of glass office partitions, light-colored walls, and open office planning
Structural System:	• Wood and concrete
Mechanical System:	• Natural ventilation and hydronic heating
Exterior/Interior Materials:	• Recycled content • Sustainably acquired or renewable resource • Manufacturing energy efficiency and recycling • Low-emissions manufacturing processes • Minimum recycled, recyclable packaging • Maximum transport efficiency • Minimum installation hazards • Low toxic emissions • Durability • Ease of maintenance • Reusability and ability to be salvaged • Recyclability

Corridor view.

PROJECT DESIGN

Ownership of the Presidio of San Francisco, with a military history spanning more than 225 years and including three countries—Spain, Mexico, and the United States—was transferred from the U.S. Army to the National Park Service in 1994. During the past 14 years, the Presidio has been transformed into a new urban national park by the National Park Service, and more recently by the Presidio Trust, an executive agency of the U.S. government. The original goal for the site was to create a global center dedicated to addressing the world's most critical environmental, cultural, and social challenges. The Thoreau Center was the first privately funded rehabilitation project to be completed at the Presidio and provides a model for private/public partnerships and sustainable development of a multitenant, nonprofit center.

When the Presidio's Letterman Hospital wards were originally designed in 1901, the buildings were planned to respond to the need for natural light and ventilation. Artificial lighting and large mechanical systems were in their infancy and thus could not be relied upon. The narrow width of the buildings and abundant access to exterior windows provides for excellent daylighting conditions and natural ventilation for the interior spaces.

The new office spaces were designed to maximize that penetration of the daylight and natural ventilation into the work areas. The office area was designed with a layering of private and open work areas. The private and semiprivate offices were located at the perimeter of the building, defined by a seven-foot-high glass and aluminum wall system to assure that both the natural light and air flow would reach the interior open work areas. The new custom workstations were designed with adjustable desks for maximum ergonomic control by the tenants.

Given that both the buildings and their surroundings are designated as a national historic landmark, the retention of the existing materials, configuration, and character was critical to the National Park Service. The original circulation and general plan configuration were maintained. New interior tenant space was recaptured by enclosing the original porte-cocheres of two of the ward buildings. New restrooms, an elevator, and handicapped access were discreetly incorporated into the original plan.

The new architectural features needed to be designed in a way that could be reversible so as not to damage the original structure if the use of the building changed again in the future. Key existing elements, such as the original windows, could not be altered. Thus, balancing energy performance against the retention of historic fabric was an important part of the design dialogue on this project.

The landscape features surrounding the Thoreau Center are also included in the landmark designation. The large open grass areas, significant historic plantings, and exterior circulation patterns are all a part of the historic cultural landscape. As such, the design of the new landscape elements must also meet the requirements of the Secretary of the Interiors' Guidelines for Historic Rehabilitations. In addition to the restoration and maintenance of the existing features, many sustainable landscape practices were incorporated into the design.

The transformation from hospital wards to new energy efficient offices is complete. The Thoreau Center is now a thriving community of related nonprofit organizations dedicated to community development and environmental stewardship. The Thoreau Center is the first privately funded park project. In today's politi-

cal and economic context, the successful completion of the Thoreau Center, without government funds, will serve as a model for the future success of the Presidio and for all other base closures throughout America.

PROJECT CONSTRUCTION

In spite of the restrictions imposed on the project by its landmark status, the scope of the renovations to the four buildings was extensive. The existing structures were completely upgraded. The work included installing new thermal and weather protection, adding new elevators and bathrooms, and completely reconfiguring the interiors into office space to support a variety of nonprofit organizations.

In addition, all of the buildings' systems were replaced. These include a new energy efficient hydronic radiant heating system, all new electrical and data systems, energy efficient lighting, enhancement of natural daylighting, and the integration of a photovoltaic panel system. This system produces approximately 2 kW of power at peak capacity or 8 kWh per day.

In addition to complying with the environmental requirements of the specifications for materials and systems, the construction team supported the sustainable goals of the project by recycling building materials and debris. During construction, the contractor designated separate debris bins for scrap metal, brick, concrete, wood, and general debris. Wood removed from the project during demolition was used for new infill framing wherever possible, while other wood items were removed and stored at the contractor's yard for use on future projects. More than 73 percent of all construction debris was recycled. This is particularly significant, given that while there is now a growing market for recycled

ABOVE: Existing conditions before the renovations began.

OPPOSITE LEFT: Main stair view.

OPPOSITE RIGHT: Detail view of photovoltaic panels integrated into new entry canopy.

construction materials, it was in its infancy at the time the project was undertaken. Thus, this recycling program required an extraordinary commitment on the part of the design and construction team.

PROJECT USE

The Tides Foundation and Equity Community Builders LLC (ECB) responded to a public request for qualifications issued by the National Park Service in 1994 for rehabilitation of the historic Letterman Army Hospital building complex at the Presidio. These two organizations believed that, within these historic structures, there was an opportunity to create a new type of multitenant center populated with organizations that shared values of environmental stewardship and social justice.

The concept of the Thoreau Center offered the member organizations an opportunity to use the funds previously dedicated to office rents to promote their missions, as well as to establish a stable real estate future for their organizations. To realize the vision for this new mission-driven center, the Tides Foundation and ECB devised a creative financing plan and ownership structure. A critical component of the real estate structure was creation of a for-profit partnership, Thoreau Center Partners, L.P. This entity entered into a 55-year ground lease with the National Park Service, provided conventional project financing, and managed the renovation design and construction process and operation of the center. The ownership entity's mission is to provide long-term office space and occupancy support services for a diverse group of nonprofit organizations while ensuring that the project is financially and environmentally sustainable and professionally managed.

ECB manages the project in a way that respects the particular needs of nonprofit organizations, enforces all lease requirements, and encourages tenants to participate in a number of community building activities, events, and outreach programs.

Involvement of the for-profit development entity also allowed use of the federal historic rehabilitation tax credit program, which, in turn, provided the opportunity for equity investment in the project, though the federal government still retained ownership of the property. The limited-partnership structure allowed for cross-sector financing, including private equity, because investors were attracted to the availability of historic tax credits, conventional bank loans, and nonprofit sector loans related to program development.

The financing of the $13.5 million project was about 60 percent bank loans, 25 percent low-interest program-related investment loans from foundations, and 15 percent equity. The qualifying costs applicable to the tax credit were $9.5 million, representing a $1.9 million benefit—20 percent of the cost—to a qualified investor. The after-tax return on equity was 18 percent. The historic tax credit was a critical element in the success of the Thoreau Center financing because it did not require a market-rate annual return or payback of the equity contribution to the project.

The combination of favorable nonprofit loans and essentially passive equity—because the returns primarily come from the credit—allowed the ownership group to maintain long-term predictable rents for its nonprofit tenants and to avoid following the speculative market rent increases during the dot-com bubble, when other landlords were compelled to raise rents and evict nonprofit tenants in order to take advantage of more favorable economic opportunities.

Typical workstation.

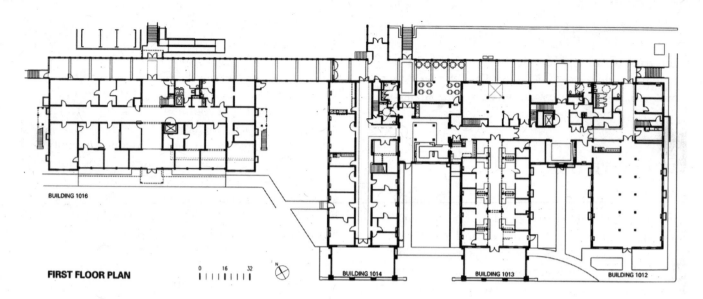

BUILDING 1016

FIRST FLOOR PLAN

0   16   32

N

BUILDING 1014   BUILDING 1013   BUILDING 1012

LEFT: First-floor plan.

BOTTOM LEFT: Typical section at building 1013.

BOTTOM RIGHT: Site plan.

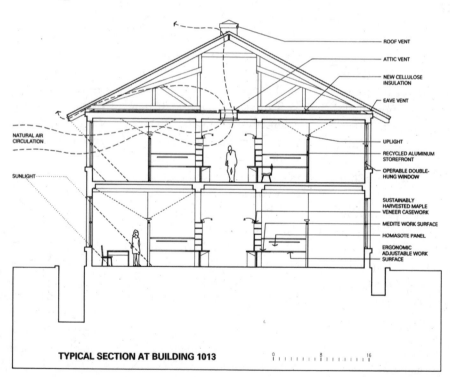

ROOF VENT

ATTIC VENT

NEW CELLULOSE INSULATION

EAVE VENT

NATURAL AIR CIRCULATION

UPLIGHT

RECYCLED ALUMINUM STOREFRONT

OPERABLE DOUBLE-HUNG WINDOW

SUNLIGHT

SUSTAINABLY HARVESTED MAPLE VENEER CASEWORK

MEDITE WORK SURFACE

HOMASOTE PANEL

ERGONOMIC ADJUSTABLE WORK SURFACE

TYPICAL SECTION AT BUILDING 1013

0   8   16

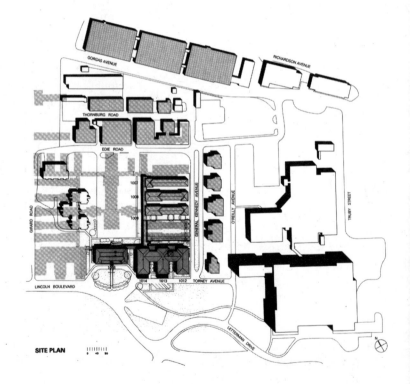

GORGAS AVENUE
RICHARDSON AVENUE
THORNBURG ROAD
EDIE ROAD
GIRARD ROAD
GENERAL KENNEDY AVENUE
O'REILLY AVENUE
TRUBY STREET
LINCOLN BOULEVARD
1014 1013 1012 TORNEY AVENUE
LETTERMAN DRIVE

SITE PLAN

0   40   80

N

160   THE THOREAU CENTER FOR SUSTAINABILITY

HISTORIC PRESERVATION AND SUSTAINABILITY

The design of the Thoreau Center provides an excellent example of the important relationship between historic rehabilitation and sustainable development. By transforming older buildings into new uses, there is a net reduction in the utilization of resources and building materials, as well as the preservation of important architectural and cultural landmarks. More importantly, building rehabilitation reinforces the concept of using what already exists within the boundaries of our existing developed areas, thereby stopping the continued development, decentralization, and sprawl of our urban and suburban areas.

The creation of this new center provides an unprecedented opportunity to showcase sustainable design principles and sound environmental practices. It also presented a major challenge in transforming the historic hospital wards into new office space integrating new energy efficient building systems and green materials while maintaining the historic integrity of the landmark structures. In addition to the rehabilitation requirements of the National Park Service for historic landmark buildings and landscape, the project also had to conform to the rehabilitation requirements for the federal historic tax credit program which was critical to the financial viability of the Thoreau Center.

Constructed by the U.S. Army between 1899 and 1933, the buildings were in bad repair and needed completely new electrical, mechanical, plumbing, and life safety systems as well as basic building maintenance and accessibility upgrades. In addition, the hospital wards needed to be transformed and reconfigured into office space appropriate for a variety of nonprofit organizations. Public exhibit space was also included in the program for the new center.

Building 1016, the original Letterman Hospital administration headquarters, is a three-story wood frame building. This is the main public entry to the Thoreau Center. The upstairs offices are devoted to "incubator space" for a variety of small nonprofit organizations. Adjoining Building 1016 are buildings 1012, 1013, and 1014, which form an E-shaped two-story concrete structure. These buildings originally served as wards, research laboratories, and operating rooms. These

Buildings 1012, 1013, and 1014 after renovation.

buildings were renovated to provide offices for the Tides Center, the Tides Foundation, the Energy Foundation, and the Institute for Global Communications.

A north-facing gallery, linking all of the original buildings of the complex, serves as the new "Main Street" for the center and also provides opportunities for exhibit space and a cafe. Site work included restoration of the surrounding grounds and the creation of the Thoreau Courtyard to the north of buildings 1012–1014. The renovation had to be accomplished within a budget of $4.1 million for base building and tenant improvements, excluding sitework (approximately $55/square foot).

The most important environmental goal for this project was to prove that it is possible and economically viable to transform and recycle existing historic building resources into new uses for the next century. Historic rehabilitation is a fundamental act of sustainable development. Other project goals included the efficient use of resources, integration of energy saving systems, and the use of environmentally sound building materials and practices.

THE ROBERT REDFORD BUILDING FOR THE NATURAL RESOURCES DEFENSE COUNCIL

SANTA MONICA, CALIFORNIA

Completed:	May 2005
Owner:	Natural Resources Defense Council
Architects:	Moule & Polyzoides Architects and Urbanists
Consultants:	Nabih Youseff and Associates—Structural Engineers
	Syska and Hennessy—MEP Engineers
	CTG Energetics, Inc.—Sustainability Consulting
	Bill Wilson—Water Design
	Tishman—Construction Management
	DLA Cost Estimating—Cost Control
General Contractor:	TG Construction
Photographer:	Tim Street Porter
Site:	Existing building in the Bayside District of Santa Monica
Environment:	An urban, active mixed-use pedestrian neighborhood that fronts on Second Street and has protected views of the Pacific Ocean to the south and west. The location is on a bus line, and is within walking distance to shops, hotels, housing, other organizations and offices, Palisades Park, and the beach.
Program:	The building's frontage is along Second Street, with an entrance to the offices at the side and an entrance to the Environmental Action Center with its windows at the base of the building. The building's retail and exhibit space amplify the busy street activity encouraged by a thriving biweekly Farmer's Market that extends down Second Street. The second-story piano-nobile houses a conference room in the center bay with offices on its flanks. This center conference room is lit by high clerestory

View toward the Pacific Ocean.

lights and is the first of the "lighthouses" that march down the center of the building. The rear of the building opens up to the ocean on the third floor while creating a tight urban face to the alley below. A cluster of village-like structures surrounds an open patio that takes in the best views, light, and fresh ocean breezes.

Square Footage: 15,000 square feet

Sustainable Features:

- Public transportation is easily accessible—two bus stations are within a quarter mile of the building.
- Amenities for bicycle and scooter riders include a bicycle rack and on-site shower facilities.
- Highly efficient irrigation system with a unique subsurface irrigation system saves an average of 50 to 60 percent in water use.
- Rainwater harvesting: all rainwater is collected and pretreated using active carbon filters, and stored in two 3000-gallon cisterns. This water is delivered to the gray water system for toilets and irrigation.
- Previous paving—the nonlandscaped areas of the side and back yard use a porous surface (Gravelpave2).
- Low-water fixtures: waterless urinals, dual-flush toilets, and high efficiency one-half gallon per minute faucets.
- Gray water recycling: water is collected from showers and lavatory sinks, mixed with stored rainwater, and treated. The system has a capacity of 800 gallons per day.
- Building commissioning—the NRDC engaged a commissioning authority, independent from the design team, in order to verify and ensure that fundamental building elements and systems were designed, installed, and calibrated to operate as intended.
- Increased building envelope insulation: R-value is increased from code prescribed R-11 to R-27 for the roof and R-19 for the exterior walls.
- Energy Star–rated, light-colored roof coating.
- In addition, heating and cooling to individual offices shut off automatically when windows are opened.
- Daylight controls—fixtures with photosensors dim light at corridors and common areas when daylight is sufficient.
- Occupancy sensor lighting controls in perimeter offices.

- Operable windows, Low-E double-glazed windows at east and west elevations, transom windows over the office entrances.
- A 7.5-kW grid-connect photovoltaic solar electric array produces approximately 37.5 kWh of electricity per day, enough for roughly 20 percent of NRDC's needs.
- For the remainder of the building's energy needs, NRDC buys renewable energy generation credits (wind certificates), making the building 100 percent powered by renewable sources.
- Rooms that have equipment that produce harmful particles such as copiers are provided with negative pressure and are ventilated utilizing separate fans.

Structural System:

- Approximately one-third of the structure is rehabilitated to meet current codes, with the remaining two-thirds of new construction using only FSC-certified lumber and steel members with a minimum of 75 percent recycled content.

Mechanical System:

- High-efficiency HVAC equipment with two-speed compressors and three-speed interior fans deliver heating and cooling loads.
- 100 percent OSA displacement ventilation design focuses cool air where it is needed.
- Ventilation grilles at the top of the light wells allow for increased air flow throughout the building to provide better indoor environmental quality.
- All users have control over the temperature settings in their offices.

Materials:

- All concrete has a minimum 17 percent content of fly ash.
- All structural steel is of a minimum of 75 percent recycled material.
- Toilet partitions are made out of recycled milk bottles.
- Recycled glass ceramic tiles.
- Carpet made out of 100 percent recycled nylon.
- Acoustic ceiling tiles made out of 70 percent recycled material.
- Bamboo, linoleum, and poplar flooring.
- Biofiber panels made from wheat straw.
- Low-VOC paints and glue.
- Low-VOC fiberboard cabinetry.
- FSC-certified wood.

View of the terrace and the accompanying trellis.

PROJECT DESIGN

The Robert Redford Building for the Natural Resources Defense Council (NRDC) was conceived as a sustainable project that would draw heavily from the cues of its immediate environment. The building is designed to respond holistically to a wide range of environmental challenges and opportunities. Examples include a landscaping plan that specifically addresses Southern California's dry temperate climate, a new urbanist embrace of Santa Monica's nominally pedestrian culture, and an extensive water saving and recycling plan that recognizes the region's long-standing issues with regard to water.

A lighthouse was chosen as a locational, metaphorical, and functional device. It is a powerful reminder of this location at the water's edge, evocative of life lived in the elements. The lighthouse is a beacon, an appropriate symbol for environmental organization. Three light wells march down the center of the building, bringing natural light down to the deepest portions of the building and creating places to sit and congregate. The administrative staff is located here in bays supporting the attorneys in the offices off the central corridor.

The interior is organized around a central spine punctuated by the daylighting lightwells. In a break with conventional law office layouts, where the partners have the best light and views, the most prized positions within the building are given over to the most shared uses: the conference rooms, library, eat-in kitchen, and upper-story porch. The generous central corridor is like the public realm of the city, meant to gather people from outside of their offices and, in the Aristotelian tradition, encourage dialogue, the exchange of ideas, and teamwork amongst the staff.

TOP: Second-floor light well.

BOTTOM: View of the Leonardo DiCaprio e-activism zone, which highlights important local advocacy issues.

OPPOSITE: View of the lobby, with daylighting from above.

The interiors of the building use the same exterior siding in the lightwells along with a host of highly renewable and recycled materials like bamboo, poplar, partitions made from recycled water bottles, and carpet made from recycled nylon. The furniture is a mix of antiques, local classics like the Eames chair, custom pieces made from salvaged wood, and chairs made from seatbelts.

On the exterior, a landscape scheme was created to showcase two approaches to water conservation within the ecosystem. Along the front and rear yards a more traditional xeriscape approach with native and adaptive planting material such as Agave and Euphorbia Milii was examined. The other approach showcased an innovative watering technique along the side yards that irrigate plants from below the root horizon and utilize water's capillary action. Despite the fact that black bamboo is a high water use plant, the virtual elimination of any evapotranspiration loss (the sum of evaporation and plant transpiration) creates a sustainable end result comparable to the water needs of a xeriscape scheme.

PROJECT CONSTRUCTION

One of the most important drivers in the design and construction of the Robert Redford Building was the NRDC's decision to pursue USGBC's LEED Platinum certification. While basic LEED certification can be achieved by focusing on a few areas of sustainability and/or energy efficiency, Platinum certification required addressing holistically a wide range of issues including site sustainability, water ef-

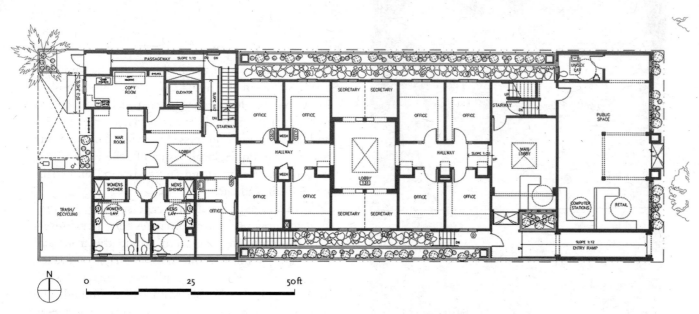

THIS PAGE TOP: Ground-floor plan.

THIS PAGE BOTTOM: Longitudinal building section.

OPPOSITE PAGE TOP: Aerial view of project and vicinity, NRDC site highlighted in red.

OPPOSITE PAGE BOTTOM: Context map.

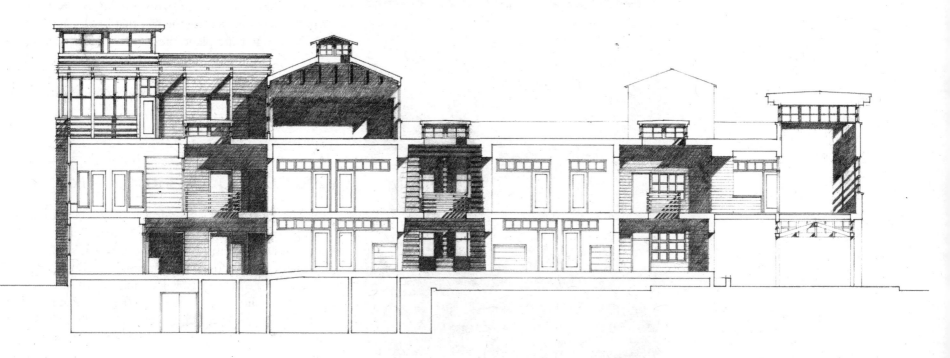

NRDC

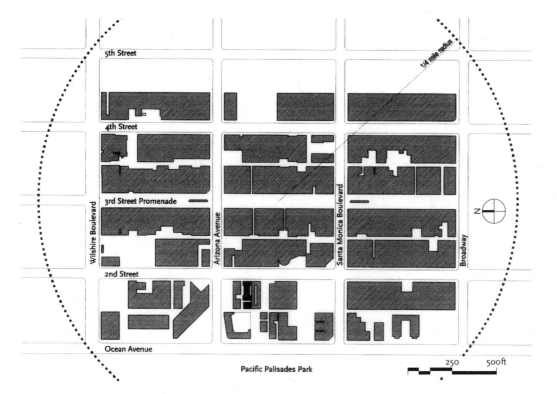

5th Street
4th Street
3rd Street Promenade
2nd Street
Ocean Avenue

Wilshire Boulevard
Arizona Avenue
Santa Monica Boulevard
Broadway

1/4 mile radius

N

Pacific Palisades Park

250   500ft

ficiency, energy and atmosphere, materials and resources, and indoor air quality.

The project is an adaptive reuse of a building that was originally built in the 1920s and was heavily remodeled in the 1970s. Sadly, much of the exterior detailing, the columns, and the facade were poorly constructed from plastic and foam so all of the facades needed to be reconfigured. However, any renovation, no matter how extensive, should be considered as a major component in a sustainable building approach.

All lumber and plywood utilized in the building was sustainably harvested and certified by the Forest Stewardship Council. The design and building team's commitment to construction waste management can be seen in the recycling of 92 percent of the deconstructed materials and construction waste.

During construction, a two-week flush of all mechanical systems was implemented to prevent indoor air quality problems resulting from the construction/renovation process. MERV-13 filters were used throughout. Indoor air quality is monitored 24 hours a day, so when CO_2 levels increase, a warning allows building users to flush out the air in the building, utilizing the exhaust fans installed at the top of the light wells.

Improved natural ventilation includes operable transom windows over the office entrances. Ventilation grilles at the top of the light wells allow for increased air flow throughout the building, providing a better indoor environmental quality and reducing the air-conditioning needs of the building.

The NRDC's Robert Redford Building achieved a Platinum LEED rating. Among these points are innovation points for exceptional performance in construction waste management by salvaging or recycling over 90 percent of the construction waste and deconstruction materials.

PROJECT USE

In addition to accommodating the NRDC's Southern California office staff, the Redford Building also houses the Environmental Action Center, which has a variety of exhibits that describe water, urban, air, and green building issues. It also includes a series of computer programs designed for kids that allow them to communicate directly with decision makers. One of the most interactive features for the public is a program that describes the building's performance in its new urbanist setting with a "real time" monitor of all of the sustainable measures in the building. One can see how much power is generated by the photovoltaic panels, how much water is being recycled, how much fresh air is being brought into the building, and the balance of natural and electrical lighting as the viewer engages the software.

The structure's performance, which was optimized during a two-year commissioning process, has met or exceeded the initial projections. The early occupancy stage involved a learning curve with regard to its operation, as some of the systems differ substantially from those found in a conventional building. For example, establishing protocols to make sure windows are closed upon leaving the office, insuring adequate water levels in the graywater tanks for flushing the toilets, and sourcing a knowledgeable local maintenance contractor took some figuring out.

With a history of over three years of occupancy and a staff of 30, the building delivers all that it promised: energy and water savings, comfort, natural light, excellent ventilation, and high indoor air quality. Most important perhaps, the building works as an excellent outreach and teaching tool, with visitors touring weekly to learn about ecological design and technologies, and a beautiful meeting space for special events.

View from the alley.

GRAYWATER REUSE

Given the growing demand for water in California and the rest of the American Southwest, and the increasing stress these demands are putting on the finite resources available, the NRDC placed a special premium on the Robert Redford Building's water usage.

In addition to installing waterless urinals, dual-flush toilets, and low-flow faucets (the conventional approach to water conservation), the NRDC and its design team also installed an extensive graywater recycling system. This system, which combines both rainwater collected in two cisterns with a capacity of 3000 gallons and used shower and lavatory water, is used to flush toilets and irrigate the building's landscaping.

Initially, the water is collected from showers and lavatory sinks, mixed with stored rainwater and treated utilizing an Equaris Infinity treatment system. The system has a capacity of 800 gallons per day. This system consists of a surge tank for flow control, an aeration tank to produce aerobic conditions, and a clarification tank to return the settled solids back to the surge tank. An extremely energy efficient air compressor provides an abundant amount of air to continuously circulate the waste water. A disinfection system utilizes ozone, 20-micron and 1-micron filters, UV light, ultrafilters, and reverse osmosis to clean water to make it available for irrigation and toilet flushing.

As a consequence, the building's municipal water needs have been sharply reduced. While the payback for such systems may not be cost effective in the for-profit development, it is a very compelling technology for institutions that manage their physical assets over a long period. This technology, like many sustainable technologies, is an effective way to conserve water, but it is also self-capitalizing.

Main entrance to the Environmental Action Center.

FORESTECH
BARNSDALE, AUSTRALIA

Completed:	2004
Owner:	Gippsland Timber Development Limited with ownership passed on to East Gippsland Institute of Tafe
Architect:	Sedunary Lake & Partners Pty Ltd Graeme Sedunary Anthony Lake Alex Prokopavicius
Consultants:	Trevor Tiller & Associates—Services Engineer Slattery Australia—Quantity Surveyor Fisher Stewart—Hydraulics Engineering Aspect—Landscape Architects
General Contractor:	NJ & MN Brooker Pty Ltd
Photographer:	Trevor Mein SLAP Architects Pty Ltd
Site:	Located in the Colquhoun State Forest between Bairnsdale and 10 kilometers northwest from Lakes Entrance, Princes Highway, Victoria, Australia
Environment:	Rural—Forestech is located in a heavily forested area in Southeast Australia near Melbourne
Program:	Staged program over 15 months
Square Footage:	3,500 square meters
Sustainable Features:	• Water catchment rockeries and collection dam • Use of local timber used at a high value end • Layout of building plan to encourage passive ventilation • Siting of building aboveground to eliminate excavation • No finishes to materials

The building follows the natural fall of the land to allow for passive ventilation and cooling.

Structural System:
- Concrete slab and timber-framed floors
- Conventional timber stud walls
- Timber roof trusses

Mechanical System:
- Natural ventilation
- Ceiling fans
- Isolated air conditioners

Materials:
- Corrugated iron to wall cladding
- Perforated corrugated iron ceiling panels
- Local timber cladding, veneer, feature grade floorboards
- Plywood (varying species) wall + ceiling lining

BELOW LEFT: View west.

BELOW RIGHT: Decks on the north side are concrete rather than timber decking to eliminate sparks or wind-driven embers that are a threat to this ecosystem.

OPPOSITE PAGE: The entry highlights the palette of local woods.

PROJECT DESIGN

Forestech, formally the Network for Excellence in the Hardwood Timber Industry (NEHTI), was to provide the first Australian-coordinated, industry-wide approach to training, research, business, and tourism-related activity in hardwood timbers. The center would bring together three disparate cultures in the hardwood timber industry: resource management, furniture design, and forest harvesting. Each had previously worked independently at separate locations. The facility is the culmination of teamwork between representatives of these disciplines including the students and the architects.

The site is nestled in the Colquhoun State Forest northwest of the Gippsland Lakes Region in Australia. The isolation of the site, although it can be viewed from the highway, reflects the nature of the forestry industry. Many indigenous species of flora that are found in this area, such as blackwood, blue box, river peppermint, manna gum, and messmate stringybark, have been used where practical in the visible design of the building. The external landscape leads into forest walks of various lengths that are self-guided, although they have strong interpretive emphasis.

The limited financing provided by the government and the requirements of the three user groups that were to occupy the building far exceeded the allowed budget, thereby creating a challenging design brief. The forest harvesting group saw itself as culturally different—a forest-based activity and not an indoor group. Part of the schematic design process was to educate and thus convince the various interest groups that certain facilities had to be shared. The process employed to convince the competing groups to understand the necessity of multiusing and sharing of facilities was a series of forums.

Given the very nature of the building's function and the integration of the building in its forest location, it was imperative that the building incorporate local hardwood timbers to the highest end value and be innovative in their design and use. As such, the fundamental philosophical design approach of the form was influenced by the traditional sawmills in the area, complete with furnaces, drying racks, and the practical requirement needed to supplement the needs of the process.

One way in which the design method differed from conventional processes and garnered exciting results was the design and construction of the reception desk by the students. This became their major design project for the year and consequently gave the students the sense that they had a stake in the design process. The result is a very well-crafted desk constructed from timbers used from the site with the added advantage of being cost effective.

The design incorporated a "street" concept, a strong lineal form that runs in an east-west direction from which all the activities on the campus are linked, providing a harmonic visual presence along the Princes Highway. This form also enabled passive ventilation and cooling and allowed the building to follow the natural fall of the land and sit below the tree canopy and, more important, to maximize the northern aspect for solar access.

PROJECT CONSTRUCTION

The construction approach, which primarily employs lightweight timber construction, was chosen to minimize the impact on the existing land form. The structural components use common bush poles harvested from the site combined with timber trusses and some steel framing.

The visible materials are all East Gippsland timbers and were chosen for their high yield and durability. The external weatherboards are yellow stringy bark, sawn radially and also harvested from the site. Red iron bark was used as feature flooring in the main entrance and corridor and "feature grade" plywood to walls and ceilings. Exposed timber trusses and furniture all utilize local high-end native hardwoods while concealed roof trusses and wall structure use plantation pine framing. The other material employed extensively in the complex is corrugated iron sheeting, which has been used for the roof and for some of the external wall cladding. This is a product that has a long association with the hardwood timber industry, especially in traditional timber mill structures, and requires no maintenance.

Given that most of the materials are natural and minimally processed, they are nontoxic with little or no off-gassing. This ensures a high level of indoor air quality. The choice of unfinished timbers without applied finishes allows the material to simply gray out over time. This also eliminates toxic gases during fires and reduces maintenance.

Care has been taken to minimize the effects of bush fires on the building. Timber fascias and gutters have been eliminated where possible along the northern eaves, where the fire threat is the greatest. Decks on the north side are concrete rather than

timber decking. There are no base boards where sparks or wind-driven embers can penetrate.

The integration of the dam on the site is there for use by the resource management students in studying wetland ecology. It also provides a natural water feature that aids as a visual relief against the forest and has a secondary benefit as a backup for fire control. The water, which is harvested off the roof, drains into rocky creek beds and then feeds into the dam. One serendipitous benefit is that it has become a watering hole for some of the larger indigenous animals, namely kangaroos and wallabies.

Mechanical systems are low technology with the emphasis on passive solar design with backup from ceiling fans and small package air conditioners for specialist areas. Passive ventilation is employed through positioning of operable windows and large garage doors to areas such as the workshop where equipment radiates heat.

The nonconventional timber pole framing combined with the radially sawn cladding created many challenges. However, the builders' long-standing expertise in timber framing techniques enabled them to address those challenges creatively, and they embraced the project and new methods of construction.

TOP: Interior—red iron bark used as feature flooring. Much of the woodwork is minimally finished.

BOTTOM: Integration of the dam on-site is beneficial to resource management students who study wetland ecology. It also serves as a watering hole for kangaroos, wallabies, and other large animals.

PROJECT USE

The mission statement's description of the building as "the living resource center" has been reflected by three fundamental elements. The first is the inclusion of timbers sourced from the site and the local region. The second is the catchment of rain filtered into the dam. The third is the use of the building as a center for all aspects of the forest industry including forestry, furniture design, ecotourism, and land management.

The small business incubators in the center have been a catalyst for new and emerging designers and small business operators to market products and systems in the local region. A former student now operates his furniture design business within one of the incubators. He is also a part-time design teacher at the center. "Coming from a logging background I have always had an appreciation of the environment," he says, "but had always thought it was a bit of waste of resources when I saw the trees being felled and not utilized to their full capacity. When Forestech opened up, I saw it as a great opportunity to get into another area within the timber industry. I'm happy that this building has been built and particularly on this site. It is a very satisfying place to work."

The campus is an integral part of the East Gippsland Institute of Tafe, and staff who teach at other campuses enjoy their time on the Forestech Campus due to its informality, its unique design, the integration of various disciplines, and its position in the natural environment. The CEO of East Gippsland Tafe says, "Forestech is an amazing facility that offers a fantastic range of specialist courses, including conservation and land management, furni-

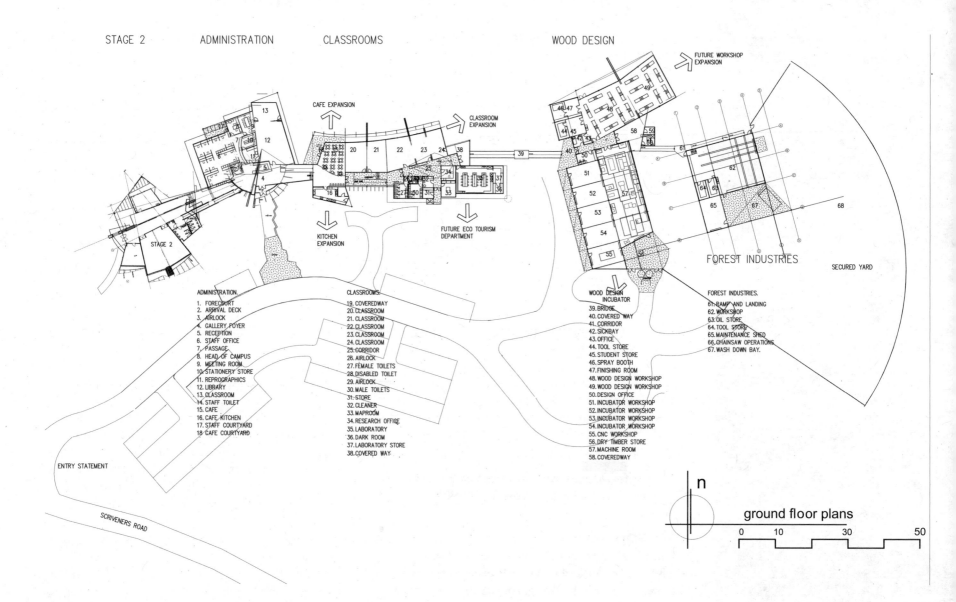

STAGE 2   ADMINISTRATION   CLASSROOMS   WOOD DESIGN

FUTURE WORKSHOP
EXPANSION

CAFE EXPANSION

CLASSROOM
EXPANSION

KITCHEN
EXPANSION

FUTURE ECO TOURISM
DEPARTMENT

STAGE 2

FOREST INDUSTRIES

SECURED YARD

WOOD DESIGN
INCUBATOR

ADMINISTRATION.
1. FORECOURT
2. ARRIVAL DECK
3. AIRLOCK
4. GALLERY FOYER
5. RECEPTION
6. STAFF OFFICE
7. PASSAGE
8. HEAD OF CAMPUS
9. MEETING ROOM
10. STATIONERY STORE
11. REPROGRAPHICS
12. LIBRARY
13. CLASSROOM
14. STAFF TOILET
15. CAFE
16. CAFE KITCHEN
17. STAFF COURTYARD
18. CAFE COURTYARD

CLASSROOMS.
19. COVEREDWAY
20. CLASSROOM
21. CLASSROOM
22. CLASSROOM
23. CLASSROOM
24. CLASSROOM
25. CORRIDOR
26. AIRLOCK
27. FEMALE TOILETS
28. DISABLED TOILET
29. AIRLOCK
30. MALE TOILETS
31. STORE
32. CLEANER
33. MAPROOM
34. RESEARCH OFFICE
35. LABORATORY
36. DARK ROOM
37. LABORATORY STORE
38. COVERED WAY.

WOOD DESIGN
INCUBATOR
39. BRIDGE
40. COVERED WAY
41. CORRIDOR
42. SICKBAY
43. OFFICE
44. TOOL STORE
45. STUDENT STORE
46. SPRAY BOOTH
47. FINISHING ROOM
48. WOOD DESIGN WORKSHOP
49. WOOD DESIGN WORKSHOP
50. DESIGN OFFICE
51. INCUBATOR WORKSHOP
52. INCUBATOR WORKSHOP
53. INCUBATOR WORKSHOP
54. INCUBATOR WORKSHOP
55. CNC WORKSHOP
56. DRY TIMBER STORE
57. MACHINE ROOM
58. COVEREDWAY

FOREST INDUSTRIES.
61. RAMP AND LANDING
62. WORKSHOP
63. OIL STORE
64. TOOL STORE
65. MAINTENANCE SHED
66. CHAINSAW OPERATIONS
67. WASH DOWN BAY.

ENTRY STATEMENT

SCRIVENERS ROAD

n

ground floor plans

0   10   30   50

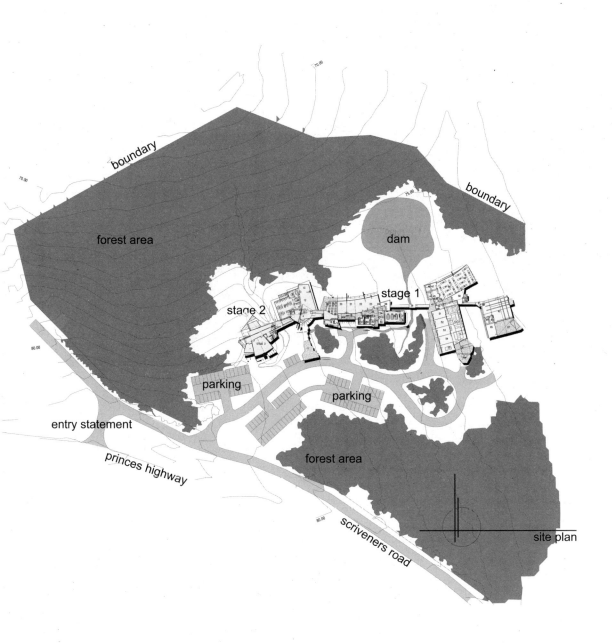

boundary

boundary

forest area

dam

stage 1

stage 2

parking

parking

entry statement

princes highway

forest area

scriveners road

site plan

ture design, cabinet making, and specialized forestry training."

Due to the passive nature of the building and the simplicity of the design and its systems, the building did not require an intensive commissioning process. Operative costs are low due to the low-tech mechanical systems employed throughout the building along with passive ventilation.

The project was marginally over budget due to the late inclusion of a lightning arrester. Building cost savings were achieved by the integration of multiuse spaces such as the café and meeting areas, thereby reducing the building area. A no-frills design with details kept to a minimum is a reflection of the overall philosophical approach to the building.

Visitors are able to experience local hardwood timber as an all-encompassing natural element from the initial harvesting through to the fine artistic furniture produced by the students. The transition of spaces from indoor to outdoors, together with the passive solar design, ensures that users relate strongly to the environment.

Due to the flexibility of the informal design and the environmental emphasis of the center, nonrelated activities such as yoga classes, seminars, summer schools, and art exhibitions, all of which operate evenings and on weekends, have been allowed to develop within the center and continue to grow.

THIS PAGE: Site plan.

OPPOSITE PAGE: Ground-floor plan.

The visible materials are all East Gippsland timbers and were chosen for their high yield and durability. External weatherboards are radially sawn yellow stringy bark that is harvested from the site, and the lightweight timber employed minimizes the impact on the existing land form.

Regional millers have benefited from both forest industries training and the research into, among other things, kiln drying schedules for mixed species timber at Forestech. A local miller has been using a CSRIO kiln for this experimental purpose and hopes to be able to dry commercial quantities of manna gum, messmate, and red iron bark more quickly than previously and to a standard that precludes internal check or collapse. "There is a growing acceptance of hardwoods for furniture making and other higher end-use building purposes," he says, "but we need to be able to produce it in sufficient quantities to replace the present imported timbers. Timber is a natural, renewable resource. Every step to improve quality opens up new avenues for use and for employment."

Local millers provided the material resources used in the construction of the building. A regional sawmill developed radially sawn hardwood siding for the external cladding of the resource center. Radial sawing of timber leads to a high recovery rate with 60 to 80 percent of log volume being turned into quality sawn timber. The installation process of the "green" wedge-shaped boards simply sat on top of each other by sliding into the recessed groove in the bottom of the wedge. Once dried, the boards shrink into a firm position and the top board is installed. It is left free of the structure to allow for further shrinkage and movement. This process also has the benefit of minimizing the warping and twisting that results from conventional sawing, therefore eliminating the need for drying and processing.

The approach of using the detailing to highlight the materials is also continued to the interior. In the gallery, where students exhibit their furniture design products, the detailing and finishes on the hardwood paneling are rendered at a higher level that relates to the work on display.

Exposed trusses constructed from local hardwoods are used in many of the wide open spaces for both their economy and their aesthetic quality. The increased structural performance of hardwood timbers allows for smaller web members in the trusses. It also allows for the trusses to be placed at greater intervals than those constructed from plantation pine. As part of the aesthetic of the building design, rough timber poles are used as structural elements. These were harvested on-site from the wooded area cleared for the building footprint. Similarly, much of the timber planking radially cut for the bridges and entry deck is constructed from logs harvested from the site.

The center also showcases local feature grade hardwood flooring in which the visible defects caused by insect attacks and bushfires animate the wood. Previously, lumber with these defects was milled for wood chips. These features do not interfere with the structural integrity of the timber; instead, they add pleasing character and texture to the finished boards. These products are now marketed worldwide as "wormy chestnut," which comprises local species such as silver top, messmate, and cut-tail.

Timber pole with radially sawn cladding.

FEDERAL ENVIRONMENTAL AGENCY
DESSAU, GERMANY

19

Completed:	2005
Owner:	Federal Republic of Germany
Architects:	Sauerbruch Hutton
	Matthias Sauerbruch
	Louisa Hutton
	Juan Lucas Young, Jens Ludloff
Consultants:	Krebs & Kiefer—Structural Engineering
	Zibell Willner & Partner—Environmental Engineerings
General Contractor:	None
Photographer:	Annette Kiesling (AK)
	Jan Bitter (JB)
Site:	Dessau, Saxony-Anhalt, Germany
Environment:	Urban environment, near the city center and main railway, in a derelict industrial area, the Gas Quarter.
Program:	Office building with public auditorium, library, and restaurant for Germany's central federal authority for environmental protection
Square Footage:	39,800 square meters/428,403.63 square feet
Sustainable Features:	• The building has been designed to minimize the area of its external skin. For those offices with an external facade, very high levels of thermal insulation of walls and windows help to reduce heat loss.
	• Natural ventilation and daylight penetration are maximized.
	• Window sizes have been optimized according to each office's specific location to profit from daylight while limiting solar gain.

Entrance to the site. (JB)

- Operable window and retractable blinds provide adjustable solar shading.
- On days of high or low external temperature a large geothermal heat exchanger naturally conditions fresh air before it reaches the interior spaces.
- The high thermal mass of the walls and ceilings together with night ventilation of the offices enables further cooling of the offices in the summer.
- The cooling of select areas (such as IT-center and kitchen) is achieved by a solar-powered adsorption chiller.
- 20 percent of the building's energy needs are met from renewable sources. 250 m^2 of photovoltaic cells have been integrated into the glazing of the forum roof and a local landfill site provides energy for a gas turbine.
- All building materials were selected for ecological and biological suitability. The most visible of these material choices is a panel facade made entirely of untreated local timber, which is prototypical in Germany.
- The building's performance is being monitored continuously. Measurements are taken, analyzed, and published in order to make the experiences of this prototypical building available for the public and the profession alike.

Structural System:
- Reinforced concrete frame structure with supports and flat slab floors
- Timber facade: prefab wood frame structure with insulation

Mechanical System:
- Mixture of natural and mechanical ventilation
- Large geothermal heat exchanger precools summer air and preheats winter air

Materials:
- Timber (larch from certified sustainable local forestry)
- Concrete
- Glass
- Natural rubber flooring
- Locally quarried stone
- Green roof

Detail of the central corridor (offices), with shared exterior lighting. (AK)

PROJECT DESIGN

The competition for the Federal Environmental Agency's new headquarters, held in 1998, set strict ecological targets. As a case study building for sustainability, it not only had to provide public services and demonstrate high standards of energy efficiency and environmentally compatible construction, but also revitalize the surrounding townscape and generate environmental awareness in the region. The architects won the competition with a design that relates the urban setting to the region's UNESCO-listed "garden landscape."

The overall form of the new building was designed such that a large portion of the site remains accessible to the citizens of Dessau as a public park. The new building is entered via the forum, a transitional, crescent-shaped space that draws the park into the building and links the complex's public areas, including the library and a lecture hall. A more enclosed atrium provides the institution's organizational center. This generous circulation space, crossed by sets of bridges, provides the visual focus for surrounding offices and a communicative space for informal meetings. While the spaces around the bridgeheads provide articulated accommodations for central facilities, the layout of the generic offices around the atrium can be varied to adapt to the ever changing needs of the agency. The architectural language of the building was conceived to match a more environmental aesthetic—one that inspires a stimulation of all of the senses.

The color concept, which has been an integral part of the architectural idea since the competition entry, supports the urban intention that the building is not seen all at once but rather as a series of smaller events. Thus, a chromatic treatment of the surface was used as a means to break down the monolithic expanse of the building exteriors. At the same time the use of color gives a specific character and atmosphere to different locations. A particular color identity is afforded to seven distinct spaces around the building.

In order to develop a comprehensive approach to sustainability, there was a close collaboration with service engineers early in the competition stage. During the concrete planning process, the concept was repeatedly optimized, further developed, and, where the application of sophisticated technology would have led to unacceptably high investment costs, brought back to low-tech solutions. Right at the start of the planning work it was decided that the energy efficiency attained during the first years of use should be comprehensively monitored. An interdisciplinary project team of various institutes and universities is carrying out the analyses. The research project is aimed at documenting the planning, construction, and measuring processes, and assessing and evaluating the energy efficiencies achieved during the first three years of operation.

TOP LEFT: External view of the forum, with glazed atrium. (JB)

CENTER LEFT: Public forum with auditorium. (JB)

TOP RIGHT: View of the internal courtyard (atrium), with operable windows. (JB)

BOTTOM: Detail of exterior facade. (AK)

PROJECT CONSTRUCTION

The desire to revitalize a significant inner city area was strong enough to justify the considerable amount of work in decontaminating the soil and groundwater. Notwithstanding the demanding ecological conditions and requirements, and in spite of the risks inherent in a contaminated site with a high water table, construction work only slightly overran the scheduled period. The costs were kept within the very tight budget of 68 million euros.

For reasons to do with economics, flexibility of use, and building geometry, the serpentine form was planned as a reinforced concrete frame structure with flat slabs (26 centimeters) and, as a rule, a column grid of 5.50 meters. In order to exploit the mass of the concrete slabs for thermal storage, their undersides have been left exposed.

The interior and exterior serpentine facades are organized into horizontal bands. On the outer facade, the spandrel areas are clad with larch wood planking, while transparent and colored glass surfaces form a continuous strip in the window zone. This glazed zone contains, in addition to the windows, night ventilation panels and glass-clad wall segments. The facade was detailed to be prefabricated. The cladding on the spandrel areas, the main structure itself, and the window frames are constructed wholly of timber.

Internal view of the library, showing clerestory lighting scheme. (AK)

1. minimising heat-loss through the building skin by:
a compact building form using the Atrium as a thermal buffer
b high levels of thermal insulation

2. minimising heat-loss through ventilation by:
a tightly sealing the building
b extracting heat energy from exhaust air
c pre-heating supply air in the winter through the
geothermal heat exchange system

3. optimising thermal protection in the summer by:
a pre-cooling fresh air in subterranean air passages
of the geothermal heat exchanger
b exterior solar protection in the tripled-glazed windows
c efficient interior-mounted shading of the glazed roof
d cooling at night with fresh air to exploit the thermal
mass of the building's primary structure

4. maximising the passive use of solar energy with:
a flexible solar protection for the offices which
allows low winter sun into the rooms
b active use of solar energy with thermal solar collectors
c active use of photovoltaic collectors

5. tempering the building climate, using the atrium:
a in offices facing onto the atrium: natural air ventilation
by opening the windows, as well as exhaust
air through 'overflow' elements into the atrium by
natural convection
b in offices located on the exterior facade: exhaust
air through 'overflow' elements into the atrium by
natural convection

6. optimisation of the use of daylight through:
a a relatively narrow building width (11.8 m)
b an optimised proportion of window glazing: ca.35%
of the exterior and ca. 60 % of the interior facades
c the use of surfaces to direct and reflect daylight

7. further ecological measures:
a district heating from landfill methane
b use of recycled material and ecological, biodegradable
and reusable building materials
c planted roofs

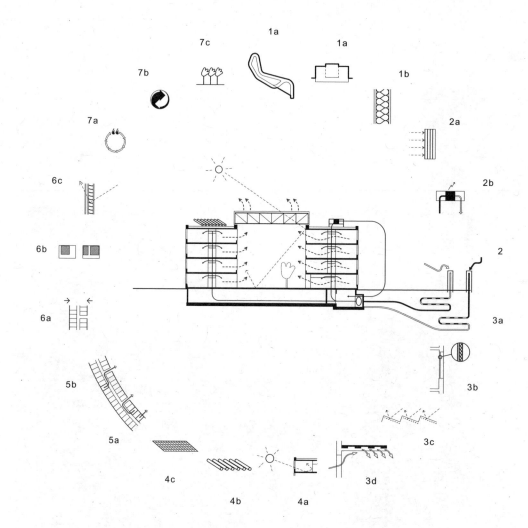

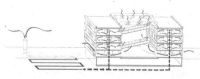

ventilation, summer

night cooling, summer

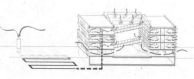

ventilation, autumn and spring

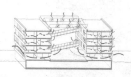
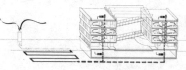

ventilation, winter

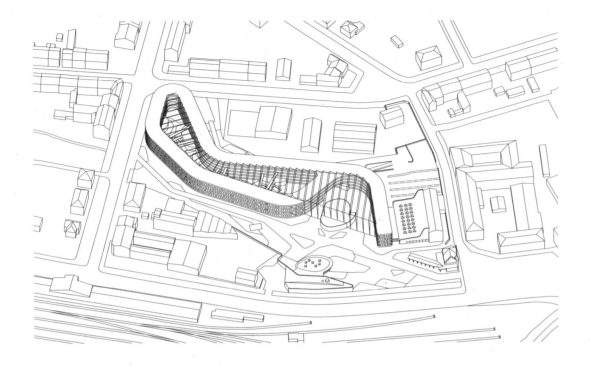

PROJECT USE

During its first two years of operation, the building was thoroughly commissioned to optimize its systems. Since this commissioning, the building has met the very high expectations set for it in nearly all fields. Currently, in some areas, it is using even less energy than the very low level originally estimated.

The Federal Environmental Agency sets examples for future projects of this kind in several respects. First, while it is a government building, it has a distinct personality. Second, it provides an innovative, well-functioning layout and a pleasant working environment that are augmented by exemplary ecological qualities. Finally, it has all been realized within the tight constraints of public funding.

The building has been embraced by both the employees who work there and the public who visit the library or exhibitions taking place in the forum.

ABOVE: Isometric.

OPPOSITE PAGE TOP: Energy concept.

OPPOSITE PAGE BOTTOM: Ventilation concept.

Annual Rates	FEA Dessau★	Average Office Building
Energy consumption (including warm water)	31 kWh/m²† (GIA)	130 kWh/m²
Electricity consumption	40 kWh/m² (GIA)	45 kWh/sq m
CO_2 emissions	29.8 kg/m² (GIA)	49.7 kg/m²
GHE§ heat energy output	124,700 kWh‡	

★Data refer to the entire complex including library and cafeteria.
†m² relating to net base area.
‡42 percent higher than expected.
§Geothermal heat exchanger.

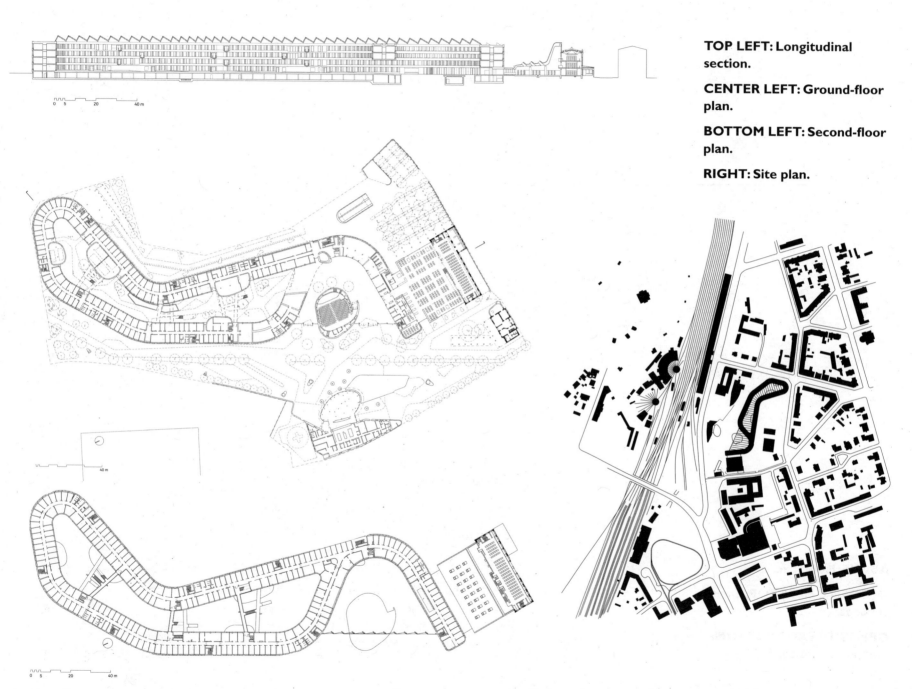

TOP LEFT: Longitudinal section.

CENTER LEFT: Ground-floor plan.

BOTTOM LEFT: Second-floor plan.

RIGHT: Site plan.

ENERGY EFFICIENT FACADE TREATMENTS

The serpentine interior and exterior facades of the Federal Environmental Agency building are organized into horizontal bands. On the outer facade, the spandrel areas are clad with larch wood planking, while transparent and colored glass surfaces form a continuous strip. The glazed zones of the facades contain windows, night ventilation panels, and glass-clad wall segments.

In order to fulfill noise and thermal protection requirements, the double-glazed windows in the outer facade have been provided with an additional pane of glass. Solar protection louvers are installed in the weather-shielded space between the inner double-glazed unit and this outer pane; these also serve to redirect daylight into the rooms. In addition to the windows that can be opened individually, there are panels for nighttime ventilation, which are equipped with centrally operated motors. These panels are located behind the opaque glass cladding. Fresh air reaches them through louvered opening in the deep window reveals. The total window area of the outer facade, that is, the transparently glazed part, comprises 35 percent.

The facade's different components were prefabricated. While this is the norm in curtainwall construction, it is less common with regard to wood components. At the FEA building, these wood components include cladding on the spandrel areas, the main structure itself, and the window frames. This is the first time that such a combination of high-tech, computer-assisted prefabrication with wood (itself a low-tech material) has been utilized at such a scale.

The inner facade faces either the atrium or the forum, and therefore adjoins spaces that are tempered in climate as well as protected from exterior noise sources. The timber spandrel areas between the window strips have been constructed as sound absorbing to improve the acoustic properties of the atrium. Sixty percent of the inner facade as a whole is glazed with transparent glass. Because the roof over the atrium has already been provided with solar protection, the windows of the internal facade needed to be equipped with glare protection only. This has been done in the form of louvre blinds that can also redi-

Detail of exterior facade. (AK)

rect daylight. The inner facade, similar to the outer one, has also been constructed as a prefabricated timber facade.

Near the access bridges, the inner facade is interrupted by large recesses or voids, which offer both informal work areas and meeting rooms occupying room-height glazed boxes. At these points, the office floors open themselves demonstrably to the atrium and so form a transition between the office zones, the informal work areas, and the communal space of the atrium.

INSTITUTE FOR FORESTRY AND NATURE RESEARCH (IBN)

WAGENINGEN, THE NETHERLANDS

Completed:	1998
Owner:	Dutch Ministry of Agriculture
Architects:	Behnisch Architekten
	Prof. Dr. E.h. Günter Behnisch—Partner
	Stefan Behnisch—Principal/Partner
	Günther Schaller—Partner
	Ton Gilissen, Ken Radtkey—Project Architects
Engineers:	Aronsohn Consulting Engineers VOF—Structural Engineering
	Deerns Consulting Engineers—MEP Engineering
	Fraunhofer Institute for Building Physics—Energy Consultants
	DGMR Consulting Engineers—Acoustical Consultants
	Copijn Tuin en Landschaps Architecten—Interior Garden Design
	Michael Singer—Artist
General Contractor:	Dura-Bouw
Photographers:	Martin Schodder (MS)
	Christian Kandzia (CK)
	Stefan Behnisch (SB)
Site:	Situated in the middle of a commercially used agricultural zone, which was devastated by intensive agricultural use, polluted, and deprived of its natural elements

Neighboring offices are cross-ventilated through open windows and doors. (CK)

Environment: Rural

Program: The Dutch Ministry of Agriculture, Nature and Fishery and the Ministry for Housing Planning and Environment needed a new building for the Institute for Forestry and Nature Research (IBN), which consisted of three branches all previously located in different buildings. (Around 2003, the name was changed to Alterra.)

IBN sought what it called a "human and environmentally friendly building for the future" that uses durable and sustainable building techniques and strategies without incurring extra costs. The challenge was to incorporate such strategies in the design and planning without allowing the ecological aspect to dominate the others. For the architects, it was interesting to demonstrate that ecology and architecture, within the standard financial constraints, are not necessarily incompatible, even when the ecological dimension is pursued seriously and not merely given lip service, as is so often the case.

Square Footage: 121,000 square feet

Sustainable Features:
- Use of green materials such as unvarnished wood, concrete, galvanized steel, and glass in the overall construction of the project.
- Solar radiation usage for heating, cooling, and lighting systems.
- Covered gardens act as buffer zones and provide shading; vegetation improves the microclimate.
- Landscaping has environmentally sound elements such as dry stone walls, trees, hedges, berms, ponds, swamps, tree lanes, and water channels.
- Rainwater from roofs and terraces is directed to a retaining pond, purified by plants, and used for watering plants in the covered gardens.
- Low-energy building due to compactness of footprint and passive solar energy (glazed atriums as climate buffers).

The interior atrium serves as a climate buffer. (MS)

- Highly efficient thermally insulated envelope; minimized technical plant (dispensing with a mechanical cooling system).
- Low-temperature heating system (underfloor heating without additional static heating surfaces).
- Natural gas as a heating medium and useful output technology to reduce CO_2 emissions (long distance heating not available; the groundwater was left untouched).
- Decentralized occupant-controlled ventilation system with heat recovery.
- Anticipated heat-energy requirement of approximately 40 kWh/m^3 per annum.
- In wintertime, maximum use is made of heat gains, making the glass buildings especially usable. In summer, they function like a solar collector and contribute toward evaporating moisture from leaves and ponds, lowering air temperatures.

Structural System:

- Simple yet open structure using wood and galvanized steel framing with wooden facades.

Mechanical System:

- With the exception of specific areas, such as kitchen and library, it was decided not to install a ventilation or climate-control system. The desired comfort levels are attained via the appropriate arrangement of a natural climatization concept. This is accomplished by the interplay of greenhouses with internal storage masses and the related nocturnal cooling.

  Heating is required only in the main functional areas, that is, excluding the atriums. The atriums are one of the main pillars of the energy concept. The building design allows for year-round use of the multifunctional atrium. Only a slight change in the energy requirement permits a far more economical execution of the facade between the atrium and the adjoining offices.

  The heating system is not subject to any restrictive requirements. Hence, an economical, easy-to-operate system was chosen for the institute that did justice to the overall building concept.

To provide heat protection during the summer months, a solution was found similar to that allowing for the efficient use of heating energy—cooling the building mass with night air. Using local sun shading (horizontal blinds) to prevent glare in the atriums and by providing adequate lateral ventilation in the atrium roof zone, the temperature in these areas can be kept to a thermally acceptable level. The office windows both inside and outside the atriums require suitable sun shading. During the summer an air-channeling system and additional ventilation openings cool the building mass by providing two air changes per hour.

Materials:

- Unvarnished wood
- Concrete
- Galvanized steel
- Glass
- Stone

TOP: The building's design is intrinsic with nature. (CK)

BOTTOM: The land was restored to a natural ecosystem. (SB)

DESIGN

The Institute for Forestry and Nature Research is accommodated in a future-oriented building with a design that embodies the efficient use of energy as a planning principle. In its compactness, too, the building provides an example of energy saving architecture. The large shielded gardens are designed to optimize the volume/envelope ratio, making the weathered exterior very small in comparison with other buildings of this size.

The east-west alignment of the facade permits the efficient use of solar energy during the winter. With their simple design, the atriums provide facile building solutions that reduce heat-energy consumption and diminish the likelihood of overheating during the summer months. The building's energy friendly concept makes extensive use of daylight to illuminate the interiors.

Functionally, woods and other materials were chosen for their environmental and cost benefits versus impact. The many factors at play ranged from insulation and glazing to ventilation and systems, providing natural cooling of the thermal mass of the load-bearing concrete. Covered gardens serve alternately as energy efficient, green working places and relaxation gardens. The building is carefully cultivated, yet edgy; scrappiness rises matter of factly above its functional, organic gardens.

IBN experts proposed a building with a closed water cycle, so the architects designed the roofs and terraces to lead rainwater to a retaining pond in the north, where plants (heliophites) naturally purify the runoff.

State building department experts used analytical and statistical calculations to compare the materials and systems used in the building to conventional alternatives, measuring the architects' choices in terms of energy consumption of the building for construction and running costs, energy consumption in production of the materials, and the costs of having the building demounted and disposed of in the safest possible way in the future.

In terms of perception of the environment, the architects wanted to convey the feeling of being sheltered in nature. Offices adjacent to the building's covered gardens (on higher levels) have a gallery for secondary routing, allowing the office space to extend into the covered garden. It seems as if the people are working in the gardens. The architects also positioned a library, conference center, and cafeteria at the south end of the office wings, as if the wind had blown them casually through the framework and deposited them as seeds.

The architects worked out an environmentally sound landscape concept which, instead of trying to reinstall nature with pseudonatural ecosystems, enabled plants and trees to naturally occur and animals to populate over time. Elements such as drystone walls, trees, hedges, berms, ponds, swamps, tree lanes, and water channels were introduced, producing a green belt linking a nearby nature reserve park in the east to the Rhine valleys in the west.

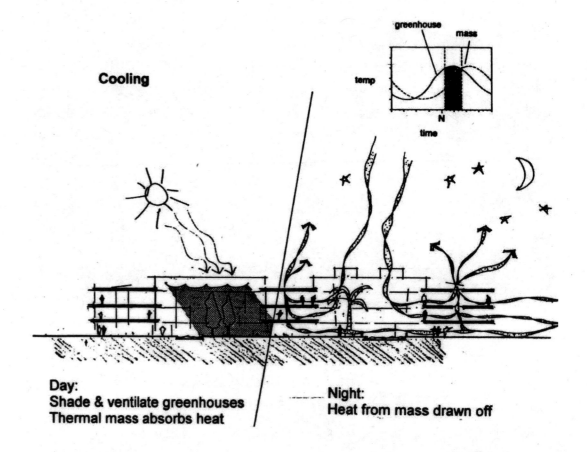

Cooling

greenhouse   mass

temp

N

time

Day:
Shade & ventilate greenhouses
Thermal mass absorbs heat

Night:
Heat from mass drawn off

THIS PAGE TOP: Cooling diagram.

THIS PAGE BOTTOM: South elevation.

OPPOSITE PAGE TOP: Site plan.

OPPOSITE PAGE BOTTOM: Ground-floor plan.

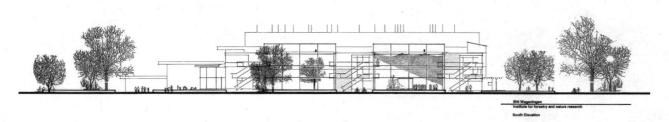

IBN Wageningen
Institute for forestry and nature research

South Elevation

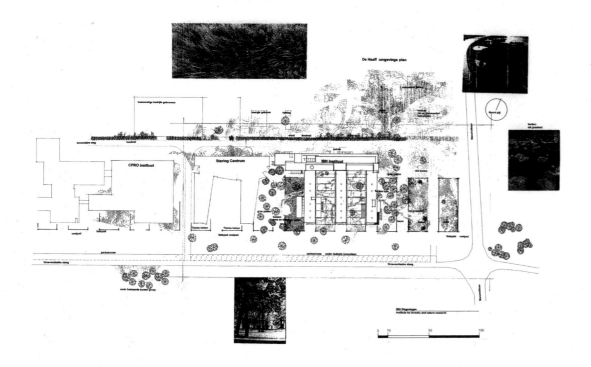

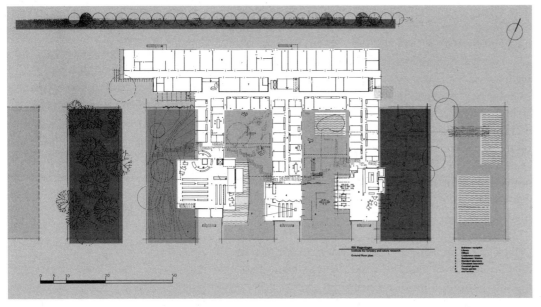

CONSTRUCTION

In lieu of a recognized standard method for calculating and evaluating ecological parameters, an investigation of the fundamentals was undertaken. This was true not only for the various materials and construction elements employed in the operation, but also for the resources and energy used, from transport to production, manufacture, service life, flexibility, and recycling/disposal possibilities of the materials, all the way to their energetic behavior. Ergonomic and social aspects, such as the question of user comfort, also found a place in such considerations.

Calculations showed that very high demands would be placed on the glazing system. Therefore, while high-grade heat-insulating glass offered the best solution for the office facade, superglazing systems were used on the north side. The atrium roof zone was executed as a single-glazed structure with temporary heat insulation. The insulation thicknesses of the opaque heat-exchanging elements anticipate future developments.

All workrooms have window openings providing illumination from the outside or from the central atrium. The light transmission of the glass used in these rooms is as follows: heat-protection glass—70 percent (total energy transmission: 62 percent); superglazing—66 percent (total energy transmission: 51 percent). The building has large expanses of glazing in the office rooms to the atrium to ensure an abundant supply of daylight. To improve the energy balance, the north facade has been partially executed as a transparent heat-insulation system, ensuring that daylight penetrates the rooms to a depth of approximately 7 meters.

The windows are equipped with glare protection and solar shading to ensure visual comfort and reduce excessive solar gain which might otherwise overheat the office rooms. Applying the principles of daylight technology, glare protection, and solar shading can be installed either outside (with the risk of soiling and adverse effects of wind pressure) or inside (risking solar gain in the room and overheating in the summer). The glare protection system can be regulated individually at the workplace. The sun shading system, which is optimally designed to reduce cooling loads and minimize the danger of overheating, operates in relation to the exposure to solar radiation on the outside and the quantity of daylight inside the rooms.

USE

Consultants contracted by the state prepared an energy and ecological balance that covered the entire life span of the building from erection, through occupancy and use, and finally to eventual disposal. The results showed extremely favorable values for the project. The report determined the environmental burden and disposal costs by investigating the masses as well as the materials and systems employed. These were then compared with the most reliably researched and quantifiable reference materials.

The energy consumption of the laboratories is highly influenced by the ventilation system. All the supply and extract air is regulated via the roof of the north-facing laboratories. Direct heat recovery is used here (but not in the smoke hoods and point extracts). Each room has its own vertical shaft in the corridor zone (hence no requirement for fireproof shutters); further installations can be added later (affording flexibility). The laboratory air-conditioning units are installed exposed on the ceilings, permitting night cooling during the summer.

The system was designed to reduce heat-energy consumption by approximately 60 percent. The laboratories are ventilated naturally wherever possible. The ventilation units are operated by the laboratory staff who regulate to suit their needs. The nightly cooling of the storage masses ensures an acceptable room climate during the summer months.

Two-thirds of the facade area of the office wings are taken up by the atrium. The rooms are supplied with fresh air through the windows. As the facades facing the atrium are not exposed to wind pressure, an exhaust-air extractor, which operates on subatmospheric pressure to ensure a flow of air through the office rooms, is installed in the middle of each office wing. Further saving is achieved by the use of heat recovery, whereby the exhaust air feeds much of the energy expelled from the building back into the heating system.

The heat-energy requirement of these areas is well below 30 kWh/m^3. Costs can also be reduced in these wings through the design of the adjacent atrium spaces. Not requiring weather protection, technical demands on the facade were considerably reduced. Furthermore, only simple sun shading is required as there is no wind pressure. The scale and performance of the heating system can be halved, thus saving 15 to 20 percent of the cost of constructing the atriums.

During the summer months, the office temperatures can be kept to a comfortable maximum of 28°C using intensive night ventilation and sun shading. Air-conditioning is not necessary.

The grid design provides circulation through open terraces that line the interior atrium of the building. (MS)

The dramatic glazed interior courtyard presents indoor gardens with extensive plantings that harbor possibilities of an almost indeterminate future. For both the outdoor areas and the sheltered interior gardens, the goal was to offer users those elements of the natural environment they need in order to feel at home.

The vegetation, moreover, supports the climatic concept. The gardens act as buffer zones and provide shading, while the vegetation improves the microclimate. The building fits into the garden structure, almost becoming a component of it. Heat escaping through the facades is trapped by the glass structures. The large volumes of air contained in the roofed gardens moderate temperature differences between the inside and outside. In wintertime, maximum use is made of heat gains, making the glass buildings especially usable. In summer, they function like a solar collector and contribute toward evaporating moisture from leaves and ponds, lowering air temperatures. The courtyards are not paved, but instead are richly planted. Extensive shading helps provide cooler air to adjoining areas.

During the winter, the atriums' double-buffer effect minimizes energy use: the loss of heat through the facade is reduced, and fresh air destined for the offices and other rooms is prewarmed. Serving to provide weather protection only, the atriums are not heated. The single-glazed roof has a series of impregnated blinds to provide protection against excessive night cooling. As a result, the temperature in the atriums never drops below 0°C during average use, and never falls below 5°C for more than 100 hours. As the atriums provide wind protection, pleasant conditions can be expected there almost year-round.

The atriums can be intensively ventilated during the summer months, especially at night, thus activating the building mass and generating a balanced room climate. The temporary heat insulation is designed to provide solar protection, too, utilizing systems tried and tested in standard greenhouses. This concept makes it possible to maintain a maximum temperature of 28°C during the summer months.

Terraces and lounges look out over sunlit green spaces. Interior plantings are allowed to grow wildly. (CK)

With their light-colored flooring, columns, and parapets, the atriums have been designed to ensure that the critical rooms on the ground floor receive sufficient light. The most critical ground floor room adjacent to the atriums has an average daylight quotient of approximately 9 percent (1 percent at the center of the room) in accordance with DIN 5034.

The areas of the inner gardens are themselves not included in the required program, and, hence, perform no defined functions within it. Instead, they offer multifarious, functionally undefined free spaces for all staff, where there are lounge areas and places for informal consultations. It is the undefined spaces that make the building especially intriguing. Since the interiors of the roofed gardens are exposed to neither rain nor wind, simply constructed wooden facades could be used. Thus emerges a differentiation between the weather-exposed outer facades and the interior, sheltered ones.

INDEX